Designing
Gardens

KLAAS T. NOORDHUIS

INTRODUCTION BY RICHARD ROSENFELD

 **REBO**
PRODUCTIONS

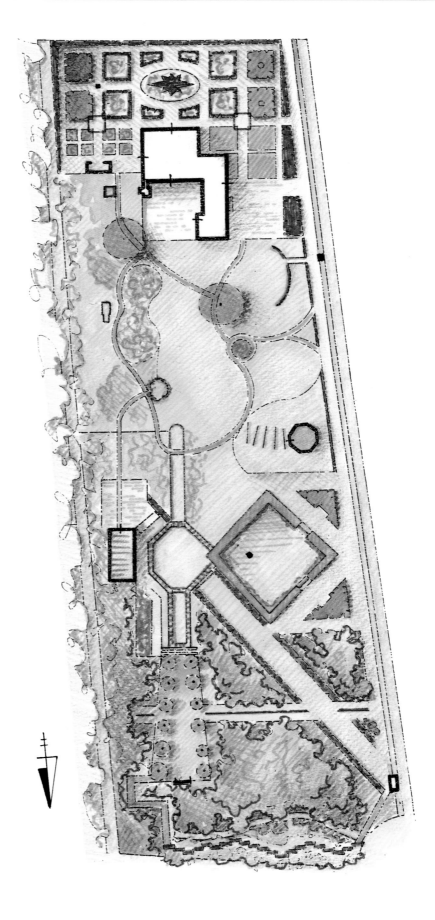

Model garden around the author's country house. This plan illustrates how a garden can be divided up according to different styles. The front garden (top) comprises a Dutch baroque garden. The middle section is a landscape garden from the nineteenth century with serpentine paths and slopes. The bottom part on the drawing has elements from the beginning of this century, with the ground being laid out in different, but absolutely flat levels. Any feeling of narrow-minded isolation or conservatory style is avoided as the styles flow over into each other.

Contents

Introduction

The best thing about designing a garden is that it turns you into a thoroughly agreeable fascist. Out you go, into the garden, Take it all in, and then start giving commands. "*You,* move there. You, here. You live. You die. I'm in control. Everything I say will happen." But exactly what *do you say*? And when?

Kick off by visiting five or six radically different, contrasting gardens, four good flower shows (one per season, noting key plants), and then start to mix and match. Plants, styles, and ideas. The qulet and outrageous. Forget the norm, ignore fashion, so long as it makes you happy.

And don't neglect formality. Kosher Italian gardens are important, sectioned with clipped box hedging, and lined with lemon trees in marvellous enormous pots. Of course you'd have to be a bit bonkers to recreate a Renaissance garden with its long pleached lime walks, and its passageways with hidden water jets to soak visiting guests, totally subordinating plants to design. Not with today's variety. But you can opt for classical topiary; for twirling spinning spirals of box, and cakestands, unless you update the geometric traditional shapes with a topiarised harp and cartoon characters. It's very easily done. All gardening is a kind of pastiche, seeing what happened before, but giving it some extra spin.

For instance, the arches photographed on page 22 could be copied exactly, or jazzed up using ideas from Monet's garden at Giverny. In his famous walk, which cuts the garden in two, running from near the shutters of the main house down towards the water garden on the other side of the road, he inserted large metal arches covered with climbing roses, planting climbing-creeping-crawling nasturtiums at the base.

I also like the dozens of ideas for paths. Gravel, brick, brick and stone, stone slabs, and look at the different patterns. Anyone can design a flower garden, it should not be terribly hard, but getting the hard landscaping right, that's another matter. It needs a very smart, clued up eye. *Garden Design* is a lively book with terrific ideas, that is bound to get you thinking. And it'll help turn you into that ringmaster, giving the right commands. An agreeable, horticultural fascist.

Richard Rosenfeld, East Sussex, 1997

Historical and landscape aspects

In my opinion, house and garden must form a unity. For the gardens of older houses, the main design can hark back to old garden styles. The history of the house and the cultivation of the surrounding landscape form the basis for a new lay-out.

The author's garden is laid out in 19th-Century landscape style (design 1989).

In the case of new houses too the design must be in keeping with the house. Austere architecture calls for austere shapes in the garden. It is also possible for colour to be in keeping with the house: a colour can be chosen for paving which tones in with the type of stone in which the house is built.

It will become clear that the garden designs in this book possess a definite symmetry. Where there is no symmetry, it is a matter of a certain balance. If we look back at history, many gardens bear a strong resemblance to the Classical and Art Nouveau periods. In both classical and Art Nouveau gardens differences in height play an obvious role.

In addition to this, we see more balance in classical gardens and more symmetry in those in Art Nouveau style. Broad paths and topiary are elements from the baroque period. There are also similarities with regard to planting between the earlier styles and the gardens in this book: the design dominates and planting is of secondary importance. Using flowering permanent plants does not set the tone – but using a wide range of plants does. The tranquillity which is created by the clear lines and the topiary is offset by the great and multi-coloured range of plants.

There are also differences from the old styles: the materials, such as concrete, iron, and glass, are from the present day. Due to the stark

lines, the gardens do not look attractive on the plans. The photographs show that loveliness is slow to "take root".

History and design

It does not often happen that a garden has to be restored to its original state. This is frequently impossible anyway as the original plans have been lost.

Also today's maintenance requirements are different. Not only because labour is much more expensive now, but also because not all machines and tools are suitable for maintaining a garden in an old style.

In many old gardens trees were planted over the years which cannot now be easily removed. Many people baulk at the idea of felling trees which are over a hundred years old in order to make the original garden style visible again. Nevertheless, some particular elements from the period in which the house was built can be used again in the garden. Ultimately both must form a unity. Old designs can work well using new, preferably durable, materials.

Even without looking at the history of a property, certain shapes of window frame or the pitch of the roof can be repeated in the garden, if they are incorporated into a pergola, fencing, or paving for example. It is precisely this unity between the shapes of the house and the shapes in the garden which will make your home unique.

Classical front garden with a star of box which is harmonious with the symmetry of the house. Around the oval, the climbing rose 'Adelaïde d'Orléans' grows along chains between the Ligustrum delavayanum *bulbs (design 1989).*

A Renaissance-style town garden, in keeping with a 16th-century house (design 1985).

History and colour

Gardening by colour is a phenomenon of the twentieth century. In 1908 Gertrude Jekyll published the book *Colour in the Flower Garden*, in later editions called *Colour Schemes for the Flower Garden*. In that book, she comes to the conclusion that it is not at all easy to garden by colour, witness the words: "It has taken me half a lifetime merely to find out what is best worth doing, and a good slice of another half to puzzle out the ways of doing it." And Miss Jekyll was eighty-nine years old! In the case of a well laid-out garden with geometric shapes, I do not think that the plants and the colour of the plants matter so much. It should also be remembered that the colours play a role only in the summer. Flower size is often even more important than colour: country garden flowers such as the peony, dahlia, sunflower, larkspur, and lupin, and more recent plants such as Austin roses do not lie easy in an elegantly laid-out garden, but all the better in very large gardens. Variegated and red-leafed trees and shrubs also have an old-fashioned charm. Silver-coloured plants with species names such as 'Argentea' or 'Argenteomarginata' are preferable to gold-coloured plants with species names such as 'Aurea', 'Aureovariegata' or 'Aureo marginata'.

History and use of materials

Not all materials can be used in every garden. In this regard, the period in which the house was built plays an important role. The landscape architect Mien Ruys used railway sleepers (railroad ties)

House in Art Nouveau style: many flowering shrubs were planted in this period.

The arch shape is in the frames of the house and recurs here in the fencing. Chives are growing to the left, Salix helvetica to the right.

from 1960 onwards. When landscaping a garden, I will therefore use sleepers only if the house in question was built in the 1960s or if it underwent major structural alterations in that period. Another of this landscape architect's discoveries was the "grit paver", forerunner of the gravel aggregate paver. She used the paver from the 1950s onwards. For this reason, when carrying out landscaping work in an older or younger garden, I will always recommend that the pavers be laid upside down. And it is out of the question to use these materials in new gardens. In old gardens, no concrete blocks can be used, and use of flagstones is typical of the period around the turn of the century. The large horticultural exhibitions of the twentieth century have made the general public aware of more types of materials: for example, in 1960 when timber for platforms and pergolas came in vogue. The trend continues still. Happily, the use of hardwoods has recently once again become taboo. The ugly colour of impregnated pine will also soon disappear due to the development of new stains.

Photograph left and below:
The shutters on this country house have long since disappeared. It would be too expensive to have new ones made. Closely tied Rosa longicuspis *now grows between the windows in place of the shutters (design 1989).*

Country gardens   Box hedges are nowadays used in gardens whether appropriate or not. The cosiness of these hedges in combination with the current predilection for over-large and multi-coloured flowers is appropriate for old country gardens. Now that most of them have disappeared, the country garden is once again receiving a lot of attention and some recognition, just like the cottage style, which sprang up at the end of

8

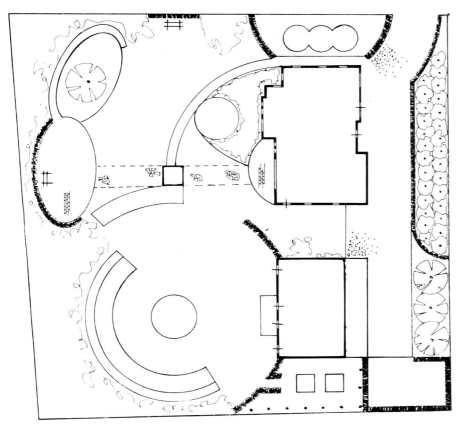

A country garden given a face-lift. On
the entrance and road side, the garden
is kept in a traditional style with flower
beds in front of the house, currant
bushes behind a hedge next to the old
farmhouse and a bleaching field with
fruit trees.
The visitor goes straight on to the vegetable garden. The back garden here
brings to mind an expressionist painting.
In this case it is necessary to think
three-dimensionally: a square construction with flamboyant roses, round flower beds with brightly coloured dahlias, a
half-moon-shaped flower bed for large-
flowered permanent plants and above
all...nothing in single-colour blocks
(design 1995)!

the nineteenth century and which became known as a "style" only when it was used in important houses. Fruit and vegetable plots play an important role in the country garden.

Even in present-day gardens, the vegetable garden can occupy a central position or can be fitted in with the ornamental garden. The Renaissance garden at Villandry on the Loire is the primary example of the manner in which vegetables can be included to elegant effect.

The pruning methods from country gardens, such as pleached lime trees and clipped yew trees, are equally possible in a new garden layout. The austere shapes lend tranquillity to a garden in which a wide range of (flowering) plants is also used.

Historic gardening

Nowadays, gardens are becoming over-fussy. Patios look like garden centres, with whole rows of pots, baskets, ducks, birdcages, and so on. The patio atmosphere from the Mediterranean area is not suitable for the northern, less flamboyant regions. Characteristics which developed long ago in the gardens of some north-European countries were of a purely practical nature. It is preferable to put just one or two large features in the garden rather than many small ones. A big earthenware pot of approximately 50cm (20in) in diameter containing a large plant is of greater effect in a garden than a large group of small pots. And what is more, it requires much less watering time: just a big splash twice a week in dry periods.

"Bramley Seedling" cordon type of apple tree. Although the trees are small, enormous fruits grow on them.

Some items which can be useful and which are of decorative value in both historically based and new gardens are described below.

Trellis cladding for growing mulberries on the walls of a 19th-century house. These fruits were cultivated even in Roman times and grow well.

Wasp trap   There is both a standing model for use on a table and a hanging model for use in a fruit tree. In days gone by a wasp trap was hung in each fruit tree in some parts of the Netherlands to control wasps. The wasps can fly through the bottom into the glass trap and then cannot get out. Sugar water serves as a lure.

Rhubarb forcing pot   Rhubarb forcing pots are made of red earthenware clay. Place the pots above the rhubarb in early spring. This will make the rhubarb start to grow earlier. The leaves will quickly push the lid up. The stalks can then be eaten.

The forcing pot can also be used for a totally different purpose: there are often power points in gardens for supplying electricity to the pond water pump or the external lighting. The plastic and the colours of these power points are incongruous. A rhubarb pot can disguise them perfectly. As the lid is loose on the pot, the power points are always easily accessible. In this way, they are also better protected against rain.

Using a rhubarb forcing pot means that the rhubarb can be eaten earlier in the spring.

Sea kale blanching pot   When the leaf stalks of the sea kale (*Crambe maritima*), a relation of the large-growing *Crambe cordifolia*, grow in the dark, they make a

10

tasty spring vegetable. What is more, the pots look good in the garden. The blanching pots are the same height as rhubarb forcing pots, but a bit narrower.

Cloche   This is a sort of large glass cheese cover which can be placed over the plants to protect small young plants against late ground frost in the spring. They were still in frequent use in nurseries until the Second World War, but most of them were unfortunately discarded when they fell into disuse. They have now once again become valuable.

Judas hole   In times gone by, many houses had a Judas hole to see if visitors were coming up the garden path. I cannot understand why today they have all but disappeared. I find it perfect that from behind my desk I can see the garden gate through my Judas hole. No visitor will escape me! If the mirrors are well-sealed around the edges and on the back, they will not be affected by the weather. They can give the effect of enlarging a garden greatly.

From behind my desk I look out onto the garden gate, which, without a spy hole, would fall outside the field of vision.

Rose box   In the nineteenth century, English landowners spent a great deal of time in their garden. Competing in exhibitions to see who had the prettiest flowers or the widest range was a part of this. The rose box was specially designed for this purpose. The prettiest roses could be transported in such a box to be displayed undamaged at the exhibi-

These wasp traps are now imported from Portugal.

Top from left to right:

R.'Reine des Violettes'

R.'Deuil de Paul Fontaine'

R.'Rose à Parfum de l'Hay'

R.'Tuscany Superb'

Middle from left to right:

R.'Henry Martin'

R.'Hippolyte'

R.'Arthur de Sansal'

R.'Charles Mallerin'

Bottom from left to right:

R.'Great Western'

R.'Nuits de Young'

R.'Zigeunerknabe'

R.'Baron de Wassenaer'

tion. The picking time for the roses was very precise: at seven o'clock in the evening. Before this time they were too far open and after this time they would be closed. There were also strict rules concerning the way they were handled. Rubber bands had to be tied round the flowers in transit.

Now the rose box is a charming decoration on the patio. According to Gertrude Jekyll, the box must be dark green. The roses stand separately in small bottles. The difference between the blooms is clearly apparent and such a display helps when learning the usually splendid, but difficult names. Place a flowerpot saucer under the box so that it tilts forwards.

Foot scrapers and boot jacks

In the past, it was not so common for paths to be paved. Only those paths which were right by the house were paved. They were often laid in a type of compacted sand. Before entering the house, the shoes therefore often had to be scraped. There are many models of foot scrapers, often in the shape of a sausage dog. There are simple designs of boot jacks, but there are also those made of cast iron. In farm houses, they were ordinary small planks with a U-shape sawn out.

History and planting

A number of flower and plant books show the dates when certain plants came into cultivation. It is known when practically all trees,

Opposite:
The majestic weeping beech on the left of the photograph only began to be cultivated in England in 1836 and, from a historical point of view, may therefore only be grown in gardens from the second half of the nineteenth century.

shrubs, roses and permanent plants were first discovered, described, or when they first began to be cultivated. It is therefore not difficult to find out which plants were grown in a specific style period. This does not mean to say that these plants are also always in keeping with this style. The Greek Theophrastus had already described five hundred plant names by 300 BC; the Roman Plinius had described a thousand by around 50 AD. In 1753, Linnaeus had described almost six thousand species of plant in his *Species Plantarum*. (For the purposes of comparison: at present there are around 200,000 described plant species.) Indigenous plants, described in herbals by Gerard, Sweerts, Dodonaeus, Clusius, and Muntingh, for example, were often cultivated very early on, as medicinal herbs, for example, but this still does not mean that they are in keeping in a baroque garden! The Gallica roses from the garden of Joséphine de Beauharnais have long ceased to be cultivated: even though they came into being in 1800 and are now making a partial comeback, they are nevertheless still not appropriate in an Art Nouveau garden. In my experience, it is not very often that such a purist view of history is adopted when using plants. The restrictions often seem too great. I would recommend a purist approach to the subject of planting only for an extremely special house where everything is in one single style.

Plants and social status
At the time of the great tulip speculation (1636-1637), a single tulip was of greater value than a medium-sized house. If a new garden is being laid out for a house built in the beginning of the seventeenth century, it is not possible from a historical point of view to plant tulips willy nilly, unless the house was an expensive merchant's house. In the nineteenth century, certain roses were set aside only for the well-to-do: only roses which had a single flowering each year were to be found in the garden of the common man. When renovating the garden of an ordinary house from the period, it is not therefore possible to use any long-flowering roses or roses which have several flowerings.

The copper beech (*Fagus sylvatica* 'Atropurpurea') and the weeping beech (*Fagus sylvatica* 'Pendula') were real status symbols: I would only want to plant one of these beeches if there had previously been sufficient land belonging to a particular farmhouse. It is not the prosperity of the present occupier which has a role to play in the choice of planting, but only the prosperity of the occupiers at the time when the house was built. Thus, up to and including the nineteenth century, differences in status had a great influence on the planting. When renovating gardens, I see it as my task to take into account the former status of a building and that of its former occupants. With regard to status, it is not just how it was in the past that needs to be looked at: I still will not plant the cheap privet or berberis in an expensive exclusive residential area. Equally box or holly hedging is not in keeping with a modest house. In so doing, I am not taking into consideration the customer's purse, but only the site which has to be filled.

Unity of house and garden

As I have already said, in my opinion the house and the garden must form a unity: the house fits only with that one specific garden and vice versa: the garden is harmonious only with the house in the way you live in it. This unity starts with the design of the garden, with a close eye being kept on the history of the house. The plan shown on the cover illustrates this: when altering the garden of this old town house, seventeenth-century features have been left intact. When choosing permanent materials (paving, garden furniture, which officially also includes pergolas and statuary), material and colour play an important role. In this relation, the country estates in which all the buildings have the same colour combination should be borne in mind. It can be seen from a distance from the colour of a farm that it belongs to a specific country estate. We do the same in our own garden by painting the garden shed or even the garden bench at the bottom of the garden the same colours as the house in order to accentuate the unity.

The garden here is focused on the living room. The reflection in the window is due to happy chance (design 1990).

Adaptation to the surrounding landscape

A garden does not have to relate only to the buildings in the garden, but vistas can also be directed towards a house or farm which stands at a great distance in the landscape. The status of the former estate can be seen from the old lime tree or purple beech. A solitary large *Metasequoia* or blue cedar is not a pretty sight in an old cultivated landscape. Thus when planting image-setting trees which will mature, take care to ensure that they are not incongruous. In the case of an old

Garden bench design for a section of the garden in Art Nouveau style. The ochre colour of the house is subtly introduced on the inner edge of the crosses (design 1993).

Contact with the landscape is clear to see here: the meadow really does go right up to the living room (design 1990).

cultivated landscape, the outermost planting of the garden must relate to the planting which occurs naturally in the surroundings. Apart from that, I do not have any objection to discreet exotic plants in such a belt. A garden is after all pure cultivation.

In an area of new houses, it is completely different: greater variation in gardens can serve here only to break up the monotonous architecture. To put it even more strongly: where there is great uniformity, it is good to use shapes and colours which seem very extreme in order to make a house more recognizable. Unfortunately the lack of unity in architecture is all too often continued into the garden. Most architects fail to adapt to the surroundings. Sometimes I feel I am more a master of disguise than a landscape architect, as I see it as my job to bring building and surroundings into a harmonious whole, taking into account the building and the surroundings.

Adapting existing gardens

From the end of the eighteenth century until halfway through the nineteenth century, most gardens were transformed into serpentine, romantic landscape gardens. Nothing remains of the old. There was no respect for the older styles; they were seen as old-fashioned. Most gardens from the Renaissance and the baroque periods disappeared. Luckily there were so many of them that a few have actually been saved. The situation is worse with gardens from the Art Nouveau period. Hopefully we shall learn from history: even now, gardens are still

disappearing which were laid out in a style which is characteristic of a specific period, purely because the dictates of fashion have changed. Restoration means achieving as great a result as possible with as little intervention as possible. Valuable old designs can be reinforced visually or if necessary camouflaged. If you buy a house which is in deep shade from surrounding trees and you ask me which trees should be felled in order to get more light into the house, I am sure to give you no co-operation in this matter. You would have been better to buy a different house. Felling just one tree in a garden is a different matter if by this single act of felling a new vista can be brought into existence. If when first laid out, diagonals were predominant in a garden, I do not feel any need to make the garden straight for a change. After a long period of neglect heavy felling is even perfectly permissible if features of the original layout are preserved, as long as they are in keeping with the period in which the house was built. It does not matter therefore whether it is a question of railway sleepers (railroad ties) and aggregate paving stones from the 1960s or a geometrically laid-out garden with or without a sunken section from the beginning of the twentieth century. Sometimes the line structure from the period when the garden was laid out can be reinforced by constructing a new terrace in the same shape or by repeating the line structure "in the air" by means of constructions or pergolas. The new materials to be used can quite safely be modern. In this way a sort of building history is created for the garden.

The railway sleeper from the 1960s is now almost entirely overgrown. A white timber construction right above the sleeper makes the shape of the original design visible again (design garden alteration 1993).

17

Enlarging effects

Every garden owner wants to get the best from his garden. By working with vistas, ingenious positioning of hedges, planting, permanent and movable elements, a garden can appear larger than it is and can also offer a fascinating view from the house.

Perception of the garden from the house

Throughout the winter and in rainy periods in the summer, the garden can be viewed only from the house. Whatever the design of the garden: long vistas from the sitting room and the kitchen give great satisfaction even in bad conditions. Of course it is not the case that the whole garden must be overlooked from one point. There must also be a suggestion of excitement, otherwise there is no desire to go into the garden. A real pleasure garden has secret gardens which you discover only when you have gone further into the garden. Such an effect can be achieved by planting diagonal hedges, which are known as en *coulisse* hedges. Of course, the size of the garden must remain visible from some spot in the garden. Long vistas are therefore necessary. For this reason, the cross shape is also to be found in most garden plans: a transverse axis which bisects the garden from left to right. To make optimum use of the space, it is best to plant a hedge at the end of an axis of vision. My aim is always to make the valuable land look as big as possible. If the ground slopes down from the house, which is nice in a downpour, you have a less pretty outlook from the house than if the ground is more or less level: a sloping garden cannot be appreciated when sitting down in the house. For this reason, lawns in garden plans are always level. In the case of dense soils, flooding can be prevented by means of drainage. If the garden slopes naturally, the various stretches can be laid in different levels. Steps and banks also lend charm to a garden.

An axis of bricks is directed at the centre of this window. The extent of the garden is visible, but the wall also still keeps something hidden (design 1992).

Amount of soil   In an existing garden, the soil is at a specific height. I try to make do with the amount of soil as it is. Transporting and removing soil involves a great deal of energy and is expensive. The man-hours spent on this tough job can be better spent on other work in the garden. In a low-lying garden a pond can be created.

The soil from the pond can be used to raise the rest of the garden. If there is too much soil, a raised plateau can be created. Such a plateau can, if levelled off when completed, fulfil a quite separate function in the overall garden plan.

For example, a raised terrace could be laid or a summer-house built on it. Steps leading to the summer-house give a grander effect to the whole.

In the gardens described in this book, the soil is never used to make banks, as banks have a reducing effect. If, when digging a pond, the raised part from the remaining soil is made into a different shape to the pond itself, it will not later be apparent that this soil came from the pond.

If the soil is left in a pile by the pond, as is often seen in landscape gardens, the pile evokes the impression of being the inverse of the pond, even once it has been planted.

Geometric shapes   A garden laid out along taut lines presents the opportunity to make adjustments later on to refine the garden further. Often it does not

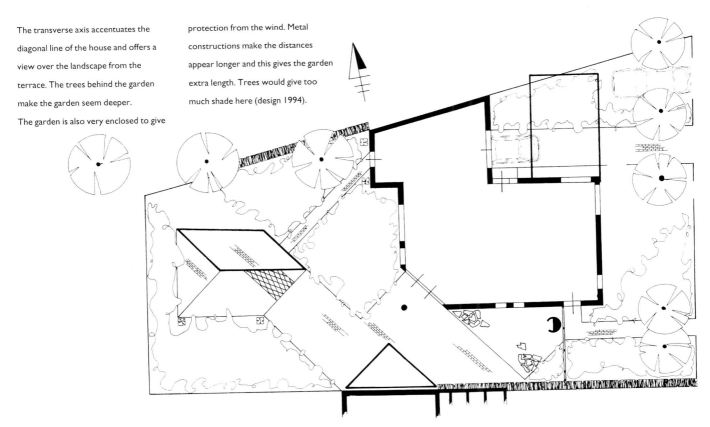

The transverse axis accentuates the diagonal line of the house and offers a view over the landscape from the terrace. The trees behind the garden make the garden seem deeper. The garden is also very enclosed to give protection from the wind. Metal constructions make the distances appear longer and this gives the garden extra length. Trees would give too much shade here (design 1994).

matter whether a pond, a terrace, a flower bed, or a meadow is made from a specific shape on the plan.

The far ends of axes present the opportunity to install many statues or pots. An additional advantage is that the tranquillity which is created by the taut lines can be offset by using a huge number of different permanent plants, which gives rise to great variety.

A garden which is basically extremely simple does not therefore have to be boring.

It is still possible to install pergolas, columns, en coulisse hedges, and so on to give the garden even more depth.

Too much finery at the initial stage is, moreover, not pretty: a better balance between installed elements and plant cover develops only when the plants have grown.

Effects which make a garden appear larger

The extent of the precious land must remain visible even at a later stage. In the following plans, this is achieved:

(a) by laying longitudinal axes in the garden which are closed by means of a hedge. A hedge removes less of the depth than a row of shrubs, for example.

(b) by thinking three-dimensionally.

Planting tall trees in a certain way or creating arcades of clipped trees results in greater depth.

It was possible to make this raised bed out of the soil from a pond (design 1990).

With geometric shapes, it is not only the horizontal plane which must be taken into consideration. The vertical lines in this picture are also repeated in the garden (design 1990).

20

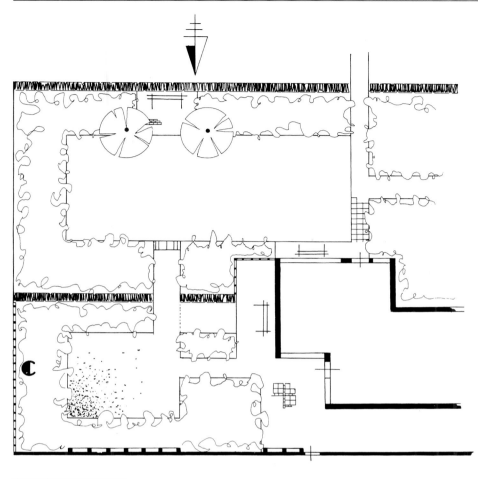

This simple plan shows elements which could still be added later if necessary. The basic design does not therefore have to be altered further (design 1994).

(c) by creating constructions which can be looked under. Making these constructions the same height as a line which can also be found on the house (a gutter, for example), gives rise to a certain unity between house and garden.

(d) by setting false perspective by means of paths which become a bit narrower further on. This can be achieved only using gravel paths or paths made of small bricks, as otherwise it can be seen from the joins between the slabs that the path is getting narrower. False must be so "false" that the narrowing of the path does not attract attention.

(e) by letting the garden run slightly downhill. There is never any point constructing banks: the bank would have to be as high as a dike to prevent people from looking in, nuisance from noise or wind. Thick shrubs are much more effective. If acting as a noise barrier, the shrubs must also be large-leafed.

(f) by planting hedges diagonally to the house. This is known as planting en *coulisse*. By so doing, the view is not restricted and the effect of a larger garden is actually achieved.

(g) by visually including a meadow or a strip of public park in the garden. When a large meadow carries on into a part of the garden acting as a lawn, it gives the impression that the meadow is a part of the garden. The same applies for plants in public parks.

Two pictures of the same garden. The photograph on the left was taken in April 1994, on the right in August 1994: a minor change with great results. Can you believe that both photographs are of the same garden? (design 1993)

21

Bad proportions in the initial stage When paths are laid broad and the plants next to them are still small, there is the question of disproportion in the initial stage. This also applies when positioning permanent plants which will have grown to their full height after one year next to slow-growing shrubs which will only reach their full-grown height years later.

Grass paths, alongside which it is intended to grow low-lying plants, must be laid out narrower than paths alongside which it is intended to plant tall shrubs or trees. In the case of low-lying plants, the broad path can also be slightly lowered, so that the proportions are still good. Box hedging, the height of which (and thus the exact proportion) is to be established later, are also among the possibilities.

Constructions, pergolas, summer-houses, and so on are visually far too big or too high in the first stage of laying out a garden. But opting for a lower item which fits in better with the scale of the newly laid-out garden is also no solution. Take, for example, the familiar 2m (6ft) high rose archway; when it is installed it will look attractive, but later on it will seem far too small and will look amateurish. When the archway is fully grown, it will not be possible to walk upright under it. The same applies to flights of steps in the garden: a 2m (6ft) wide flight of steps will in fact actually look narrow between fully grown plants!

Enlarging effect once the plants have grown Laymen think that a garden gets smaller when the plants begin to grow. That can indeed be the case in a badly designed garden or with

Below left: In the initial stage the path looked far too wide (design 1989).

Below right: This arcade of water pipes looks far too high. The proportions will be right only when it is fully covered with roses (design 1993).

an incorrect planting plan. With a well-conceived line plan and long vistas, plant growth has the opposite effect: the axes become longer over the years.

In all plans, the garden will thus "grow larger" as the plants grow: an effect of depth is produced just as the narrowing effects grow in. Even in an existing garden, a new arcade of columns can give a greatly enlarging effect. Compare this with the construction of a house: when the walls are up, but the ceilings are not yet in, the house looks small and poky. The ceilings, which have to be looked under and which give rise to a different incidence of light, produce the larger-looking rooms.

The same applies to the garden: the possibility of being able not only to look between something, but also to look under something, such as tall trees or a construction with climbing plants, can result in a greatly enlarging effect.

Cost Good design has nothing to do with (high) costs: if a certain area is to be made into a terrace, this terrace can just as well be made using ordinary gravel rather than marble. The same applies for a shrub area: planting a woodland garden costs a completely different price to planting particular slow-growing shrubs. Depending on the budget, a pond can be made from concrete, from a pre-moulded glass-fibre tank, or from pond-liner. When selecting materials, it must always be

It is hard to imagine that these 8m (26ft) steps are in a recently laid-out garden. In this garden, the gigantic steps do not look too big at all (design 1992).

Sandstone is preferable in a baroque-type setting (design 1989).

taken into account how much time they take to use. This is especially so if the construction of an item is being contracted out. A great deal of the expense associated with a garden is dependent on the third-party man-hours to be used.

Most plans show where statuary can be placed. The photograph shows a bronze by the artist Nelleke Allersma with an Abies procera *and a* Fraxinus excelsior *'Aurea' in the background.*

Art in the garden

Statuary was used in various old garden styles. Such statuary was in keeping with the period and thus with the style of garden. Nowadays, gardens still need statuary, sculptures, or models which are in keeping with the period, the surroundings, or the construction period of the house. It is a pity that so much money is now wasted on kitsch, whereas a well-positioned garden statue or flower bowl lends greater effect than many small elements.

For this reason, all plans show where a large item can be positioned. It is precisely these elements which make a garden personal: I never give advice on this matter. My designs do, however, offer the opportunity to use these sites, which have been reserved for art, for a rabbit hutch, swing, large flower pot, garden bench, a sundial, or a collapsible washing line.
In history-based gardens, close attention must be paid to the materials to be used. Portland cement was first used for garden ornaments in the second half of the nineteenth century. In gardens from before this period, it is therefore preferable to use sandstone vases.

A modern formal garden.
This plan of a town garden in the centre
of Amsterdam shows how water can be
used to form a central feature of a garden. The formal water garden is defined
on both sides by clipped yew trees
(design 1994).

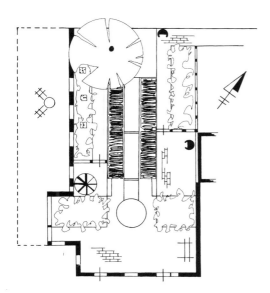

Water in a garden

Where gardens are in a flat region, it is practical to introduce height differences only if there is surplus soil which would otherwise have to be transported away. If height differences have been introduced into the garden, water courses with waterfalls can be constructed. A virtue is thus made of necessity. Waterfalls or fountains work particularly well in town gardens: background noise from the town can no longer be heard due to the noise of the water. My experiences of pumps have been only bad – they require rather a lot of maintenance. A pond can quickly empty due to water splashing or being blown away and, depending on the quantity of algae growth, filters have to be cleaned frequently.

A small torso in a large garden is provided with a sheet of glass for a "frame", thus showing the statue to better effect (design 1991).

Use of materials

The greatest item of expenditure in a garden is the building materials for the driveway, paths, terraces, pergolas, ponds, and so on. The plants are hardly a factor at all with regard to cost and installation time.

In the gardens which are discussed in Chapter 5 onwards, materials such as concrete and metal are usually used, whereas in the case of older houses, bricks and (painted) timber are used more often. In all these cases, it is a question of durable materials: after all, a garden is laid out only once. With regard to maintenance, people think mostly of mowing the grass and pruning shrubs, but the materials used to make the permanent elements can also require a lot of maintenance. Using shoddy materials for permanent elements leads only to more

expense in the long run, as maintenance work on these elements often has to be carried out by third parties. Glass is a maintenance-free material which is also suitable for the garden. It should be remembered that birds can fly into it: frosted glass is therefore preferable in the garden. Laying glass horizontally, as a tabletop or as a base for a statue avoids these problems.

Paving It can clearly be seen from the plans that the paths are usually broad. If the composition is good on the plan, it will also turn out well when put into practice. Relatively broad paths are attractive even in small gardens. When the paths are laid, the garden will look rather stony initially, but as the plants grow, the good proportions previously shown on the plan will develop spontaneously. This seems strange to people who are laying out a garden for the first time, but it should be remembered that narrow little paths look amateurish and will be a source of regret later.

In the case of large areas, the colour of the materials must not be striking. It is only the plants, not the paving, which must later attract the attention. Small pebbles can be used for small paths: larger areas need larger materials such as brick cobbles or paving stones. The larger a terrace or path, the larger the paving stones. The cutting edges – the chamfered side edges of the paving stone, for example – must preferably be out of sight. For driveways used by cars, cutting edges do of

Grass-protecting pavers form an inexpensive, but good bank support where there is a difference in height. New concrete is not pretty yet, but after a year algae will grow on it and after a couple of years, lichen will also appear.

*Opposite:
Reversed paving stones, here laid in blocks of four and edged with bricks, give a tranquil appearance (design 1986).*

course have a clear function, as they distract the eye from slight dips, which often occur in a drive. As a rule pavers laid upside down are prettier than the upper side of the pavers. The underside of pavers with straight edges gives a more tranquil appearance. The underside is also rougher, so that algae will grow more slowly in the shade.

It is not only with paving, but also when using narrow or broad edging made of concrete, that the fixed straight edges are prettier than the "real" upper sides with sloping edges. The grey colour of new concrete will become colourful within a few years due to algae and lichen and it will very quickly be possible to apply the description of "old" to it. There is, therefore, no need to buy coloured concrete. In order to obtain colour, fired bricks can be used for a pattern. Fired bricks are usually preferred to concrete, but are of course much more expensive.

Reusing existing materials

Any change to an existing garden has a certain penalty: even though we live in a throw-away society, I prefer to reuse most existing materials. It is only with railway sleepers (railroad ties) that I have real difficulty, but these can still serve as reinforcement for a new pond to be built or as steps when constructing a flight of steps. If pavers are laid on top, the sleeper can no longer be seen.

Aggregate slabs are not appropriate for gardens from before 1950 and from after 1970. Turning these pavers over is one possibility. Any dullness disappears when they are combined with bricks. The only time when it is impossible to reuse pavers is if they are ribbed on the underside. The undersides of pavers and bricks are rougher and are therefore prettier and also more practical for garden use: they are less quick to become slippery due to the growth of algae. Any old stones which are left over can be used to build little walls or pedestals for statues. You will not find any stone walls in the plans: stones are not meant for this purpose.

It is often attractive and cheap to use second-hand materials. Use the materials only for the purpose for which they are intended or use them so that the original use is not obvious. A roofing tile will always be a roofing tile, for example. Reusing roofing tiles for shed roofs, or lean-tos for fire wood is excellent, but I do not find it beautiful to use them on a garden wall or as edging. A roofing tile is not meant for this purpose.

Constructions in the garden

As already mentioned, the possibility of being able to look under something gives depth. The use of tall trees is very suitable for this purpose, but often there is not enough space for this. It goes without saying that trees are particularly unsuitable in smaller gardens in which it is also hoped to incorporate a sun terrace. Nevertheless, in gardens in urban areas, where neighbours can often look into the garden from above, something must be done for the sake of privacy. Trees have still got to grow and the end result takes years to achieve.

Pergolas   With pergolas, you are fully in control of the dimensions. You can adapt length, width, and height to the scale of the garden. This means that the model can also be adapted to shapes which exist on the house. In one case, the construction stands in a garden with taut shapes. These shapes can be further accentuated by using closely tied climbing plants. In a romantic garden, the climbers could stretch out in a rugged and wild fashion.

A pergola is not an elegant object in itself: it is only the combination with climbing plants which makes the pergola elegant. It is important that the construction of the pergola is durable enough so that after a few years, when the climbers are just fully grown, it does not have to be replaced.

The plan shows the size of construction which is necessary on the horizontal plane. But it is necessary to think in three dimensions. If there is an extension on a building, then the height of the extension can be used for the pergola. The height of the gutter or of the window-sill on the first-floor windows is sometimes used. Initially, the construction may look far too tall. When, after a few years, all the plants in the garden have grown, the construction which first looked too tall will look just right. For this reason, constructions for climbing plants must have a minimum height of 3m (10ft). In the Renaissance, arcades were even between 3.6m (12ft) and 4.5m (14^1/$_2$ft), and these gardens were not really so big, even in the Netherlands.

A construction more than 5m (16ft) high. The shape matches the roof of a summer-house which is further down the garden (design 1990).

This veranda gives protection against the cold north wind. The colour matches the basic colour of the house (design 1989).

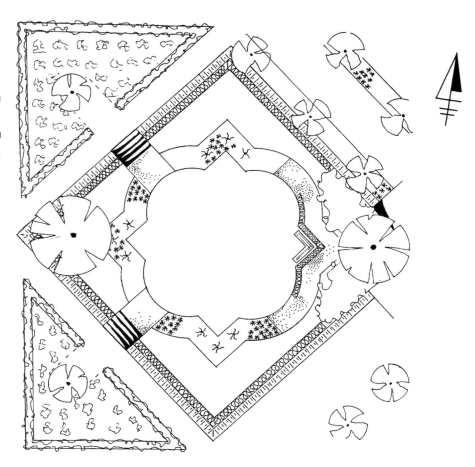

Art Nouveau garden. The edges are filled in with multi-coloured and mostly large-flowered permanent plants. Gardening in single-coloured blocks had not yet become established in the Art Nouveau period. Croquet can be played in the lawn in the middle. This game was very popular at that time (design 1992).

Summer-houses and verandas

A lot of work has to be done in a garden. Sitting peacefully now and again in the garden is one of the pleasures of gardening. Ideally, there is a pretty spot for each moment of the day, such as a terrace in the sun to catch the first rays of sunshine in the spring, and a terrace in the shade for hot summer days. Particularly in coastal areas, a little spot out of the wind is no excessive luxury. For this reason, people used to build summer-houses, which also raised the social standing of the owner. They fell into disuse with the arrival of the telephone, which could not be heard in the summer-house. With the introduction of the portable telephone, the summer-house is making a come-back. They can be bought in all shapes and sizes from garden centres.

When I am called in to make changes to a garden, there often seems to be an old shed or garage in the garden. Sometimes I get there too late: the shed has already been broken up, as it had not occurred to the owners that the shed would fit into the new garden lay-out just splendidly.

When adapting the garden design, often simple solutions can be devised: a sort of veranda can be created by removing a wall. In the case of a garage, the doors can be placed a few metres inside, so that a pleasant awning is created which is sure to look pretty in combination with climbing plants against the wall. And what is more, garden furni-

ture made of wood or cane will suffer much less from the weather when it is under an awning.

The trellis cladding and the climbing plants are also reflected in the table.

Garden lighting

I am often asked to give advice on garden lighting. I can be quite brief here. Lighting can be useful, but it cannot serve as decoration.

During the day, lamps in a garden are always ugly. Nostalgic lanterns with or without ladder supports are not objects for the garden. An exception in the area of lighting can be made for patio gardens. These are often a continuation of the sitting room.

Lighting which is discreet during the day can have a pleasing effect here.

Lighting used to deter intruders can also be used as garden lighting. This type of lighting (with a sensor), hidden away in a construction by a path near the front door, is also very practical for the owner.

Use can also be made of reflected light by shining a beam of light on water. In my own garden a glass table stands under a spotlight, which indirectly shines onto the tree above.

Incongruous garden elements

Whims of fashion do not belong in a good garden design: the house and the surroundings dictate what must happen in the garden and not the women's journals and the gardening magazines.

Following pages: Landscape style in the author's garden.

Remodelling of the garden of a 19th-century house on one of the West Friesian islands: a longitudinal axis leads to the back door of the house with a central section which comprises a metal construction with a pond underneath.

An existing garden shed forms the basis for the transverse axis. The overall design is not symmetrical, but it is balanced (design 1994).

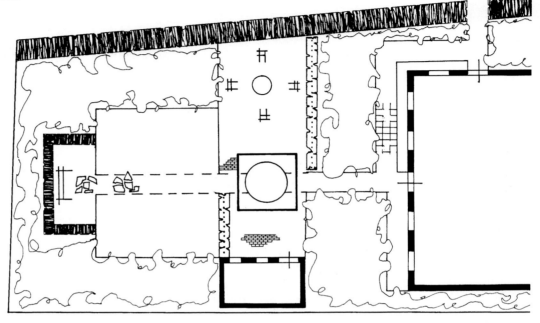

Left and right: The difference can clearly be seen here between the "natural" wood colour and the painted construction (design 1993).

English garden benches, for example, belong in England. The natural wood with the beautiful silver colour is in keeping with the old country houses and the natural stone which was frequently used to build them; while, as I mentioned earlier, the Dutch have been inclined since time immemorial to paint garden furniture, which also makes it easy to keep clean. Moreover, natural wood does not go with modern austere architecture with balanced colours.

For this reason the garden bench at the bottom of the garden or the lean-to shed should be painted in the colours of the house. That is what used to be done: all houses which belonged to a country estate were painted in the same colour combination, so that the extent of the country estate in question was absolutely clear to a stranger. Particularly in a small garden, the repeated colours are so restful.

Grey plastic drainpipes do not need to be painted as far as maintenance is concerned. The grey colour does not, however, occur in the rest of the garden and is therefore incongruous. The drainpipes should be painted in a colour which is also used for the house or elsewhere in the garden. In almost every garden, I point out this clash, which can so easily be resolved.

Planting

Every gardener has his or her own

preferences where plants are concerned.

I too have clear favourites which appear

in most of my garden designs and which

I mention under their various categories.

Plants which are often used

I mainly prefer plants which do not have a time when they are less attractive. Certain plants are popular because they make good cut flowers or they can become established in sites which are less than ideal. There are also plants which flower extremely early or in contrast extremely late. Small gardens which you also wish to enjoy from the house during the winter require a good balance between deciduous and evergreen plants. Whether or not tender plants are used depends on your own taste and dedication. As a rule I do not use them much.

Trees

With regard to trees, you have to go through the entire list of tree species and varieties for each garden plan. The spot where the plants have to go often has so many limitations that it usually looks as though only three species can be used. Favourite trees are thus practically out of the question. A cultivated form of the very pretty-flowering tree species (*Prunus avium* 'Plena'), which is indigenous to Europe, is often used in the garden plans discussed in this book because of its blossom and rapid and vigorous growth.

I frequently use the following trees: *Carpinus betulus* 'Fastigiata' (clipped form), *Corylus colurna* (medium-sized gardens), *Prunus avium* 'Plena' (medium-sized gardens), *Pterocarya fraxinifolia* (very large gardens), and *Sophora japonica* (small gardens).

Shrubs

I use a great variety of shrubs in every garden. I prefer shrubs which

Aucuba japonica *'Rozannie' is a female variety: the berries remain on the plant for a long time. There are several green-leafed aucubas. As far as I know, of these only* A.j. *'Longifolia' is male and therefore does not produce berries.*

flower extremely early and extremely late. Most people do in fact plant the usual spring-flowering shrubs in the garden. Shape and autumn colours also play an important role when choosing shrubs. Fragrance and berry formation need to be taken into account too in some cases. I frequently use the following shrubs: *Aucuba japonica* 'Rozannie', *Euonymus alata, Fothergilla major, Fuchsia magellanica, Hydrangea arborescens* 'Annabelle', *Ilex crenata, Philadelphus* (small-flowered single varieties), *Prunus laurocerasus* 'Caucasica', and *Viburnum bodnantense* 'Dawn'.

Woody plants requiring trimming

In order to create tranquillity in a garden, trimmed and clipped shapes are often necessary, especially if there are a lot of species of flowering permanent plants. Larger stretches of a particular shade of green provide balance. Clipped plants are not dull as they can also be trimmed into shapes: *Carpinus betulus* 'Fastigiata' is good for columns; *Fagus sylvatica* for hedges with niches; *Crataegus trees* can become spheres on a trunk; *Lonicera* can be trimmed into irregular shapes and the various strains of box offer unrivalled opportunities, from animal figures to cubes and cylinders.

Carpinus betulus 'Fastigiata', planted here between windows, lends atmosphere to a house. This compensates for the loss of the previous shutters (design 1989).

I frequently use the following plants: *Crataegus, Lonicera nitida* and varieties, *Buxus sempervirens* 'Rotundifolia', *Ilex aquifolium* 'Pyramidalis', *Taxus baccata, Fagus sylvatica*, and *Carpinus betulus* 'Fastigiata'.

Conifers Conifers do not assume any importance in the gardens discussed in this book. Admittedly, some species are an important addition to the small range of good evergreen shrubs. The spreading Chinese juniper bushes, *Juniperus x media* 'Pfitzeriana', are suitable for gardens from the beginning of this century. *Thuja plicata* is good for providing privacy quickly. On acid soils, some conifers make good ground cover.

I frequently use the following conifers: *Juniperus virginiana* (the species!), *J. horizontalis* 'Repanda', and *Thuja plicata* and varieties (as hedging).

Rose garden with old-fashioned pink roses at the Oosterhouw country house (design 1989).

Permanent plants It is a primary requirement to stagger flowering times in a garden: certain very early-flowering and other very late-flowering plants therefore appear in most of the garden plans. I know of hardly any set combinations, as the gardens and the wishes of their owners are too diverse for that. In order to break up austere lines a little, I often use foliage plants such as *Astilboides*, *Darmera*, *Rheum*, and *Rodgersia* in the garden plans, as well as *Asarum europaeum*, *Cornus canadensis*, *Hosta* (large-leafed varieties), *Primula vialii*, *Rheum palmatum*, *Saxifraga cortusifolia*, and *Symphitum grandiflorum*.

Ornamental rhubarb is not only an attractive foliage plant, but it also flowers magnificently after a couple of years.

Roses Of the old-fashioned varieties of roses, the shrub roses are often ugly. The most commonly used hybrid tea roses look rather formal. Not many walls are suitable for climbing roses. This leaves the single-

37

The dwarf dogwood (Cornus canadensis) is an ideal ground cover plant for partial shade. This plant is sold more often in nurseries than the rare indigenous Cornus suesica.

bloomed shrub roses which can be positioned between permanent plants. Single-bloomed long-flowering roses: 'Dainty Bess', 'Sally Holmes', and 'White Wings'. Only a few of the old-fashioned strongly scented shrub roses are long-flowering. The best is 'Stanwell Perpetual'. Of the climbing roses, the long-flowering 'New Dawn' is the best. Weeping standard roses: 'Dorothy Perkins', 'Excelsa', 'Schneewitchen', and 'White Dorothy'. Standard roses must be cut back hard, not the case with weeping standard roses – one reason for using them more. Weeping standard roses are also more resistant to frost. The cut-back bare trunks of standard roses look unattractive in the spring.

Climbing plants

When drawing up a planting scheme, I start with the trees. Then come the climbing plants. Climbing plants are extremely good at successfully merging house and garden to create unity. There are plenty of possibilities for east- and west-facing walls, but north- and south-facing walls present many difficulties. The species mentioned below are suitable for these problem walls and therefore often appear in the planting schemes: *Aristolochia* (north), *Campsis radicans* (south), *Clematis montana* (all aspects), espalier apricot or espalier peach (south), espalier morello cherry (north), *Hydrangea petiolaris* (north), and *Lonicera japonica* (north).

Ugly sheds must be camouflaged: *Clematis vitalba* provides the fastest solution.

Rosa 'Sally Holmes'. The stamens of single-flowered roses are a delight to see.

Bulbs and tubers

Lilium martagon (common Turk's-cap lily) tolerates deep shade and is suitable for the heaviest clay soil.

When bulbs find conditions to be to their liking and therefore spread vigorously, especially on clay soil, the results are spectacular. I generally recommend bulbs which are suitable for naturalizing: *Crocus tommasinianus* (wild crocus), *Crocus vernus* (spring crocus), *Galanthus elwesii*, *Hyacinthoides hispanica* (Spanish bluebell), *Hyacinthoides non-scripta* (English bluebell), *Iris reticulata* 'Harmony', *Lilium martagon* (common Turk's-cap lily), *Narcissus poeticus* (poet's or pheasant's eye narcissus), *Ornithogalum nutans* (nodding star of Bethlehem), and *Scilla sibirica*.

Under the old maple tree lies a square-shaped flower-bed planted with Hedera helix 'Goldheart', among which flowers the Spanish bluebell (design 1990).

Tub plants

The first ground frost in autumn costs many tub plants their lives as people forget to bring them inside early enough. With *Olearia haastii*, *Poncirus trifoliata*, and *Viburnum tinus* this is not a problem. And what is more, these plants like to be put outside again early.

Ferns

As far as ferns are concerned, I prefer the striking, evergreen species. These include many *Polystichum* species, the shield ferns. The ostrich fern *(Matteucia)* is not evergreen, but the fertile fronds turn dark brown in winter when they have died off and then stand proudly erect. The indigenous *Blechnum spicant* thrives well in many sites as a ground-cover plant. The polypody *(Polypodium)* can be grown in damp conditions on roofing tiles. I frequently use the following ferns: *Blechnum spicant*, *Matteucia struthiopteris*, and *Polystichum setiferum*.

Polystichum setiferum, the soft shield fern, gives atmosphere to a shady spot in a town garden and is also evergreen.

39

Water plants — Unfortunately, it is often only the ugly 'Multiplex' variety of the beautiful marsh-marigold *(Caltha palustris)*, with its full flowers, which is supplied. Close attention should therefore be paid when buying. As far as water plants are concerned, the foliage and flower colour of the pickerel weed are unbeatable. I frequently use the following water plants: *Caltha palustris*, *Lysichiton americanum*, *Lythrum salicaria* 'Robert', and *Pontederia cordata*.

Plants which do not fall into a single category — Like the ferns, *Equisetum telmateia* and *E. sylvestris* are primitive plants which create a special atmosphere. These plants offer great possibilities for a damp, humus-rich garden. It must, however, be remembered that they are rampant spreaders. Their availability also often leaves much to be desired.

Plants which are not often used — If a plant is beautiful for only a short part of the year and is downright ugly for the rest of the time, it is not worth using. The well-known *Forsythia* flowers for two weeks of the year. For the remaining fifty weeks, this shrub's ugly bundle of sticks is not a pretty sight in the garden. The same applies for the Japanese flowering cherry.

Golden rod and Michaelmas daisies often have mildew on the foliage, which is why they will not be found in the garden plans in this book. In view of the damage from mildew and greenfly, I do not use many roses in town gardens. Lack of resistance to frost is another reason for

The yellow or white marsh-marigold (Caltha palustris) *is a primitive plant which tolerates water up to a depth of 10cm (4in).*

not using certain plants. I use plants with variegated leaves sparingly: if they are used, I select only the silver-coloured varieties.

Nurserymen who grow the *Stephanandra incisa* 'Crispa' and the *Ilex crenata* 'Convexa' should realize that these monstrosities are not at all beautiful in the garden.

If you do not like the shape of a shrub, you can consider pruning it into shape. You can see from the photograph how pretty it can be.

Trees   Only a few species of tree are suitable for any one site. For this reason, now and again I have to plant a tree which is definitely not my preferred choice.

Poplars *(Populus)* lift paving with their roots and their branches are also easily broken. Admittedly, poplars are the cheapest trees to buy, but after twenty years it becomes apparent that felling is an expensive business and the timber is worthless!

I said earlier that I did not find the bundle of sticks structure of the Japanese cherry *(Prunus)* pretty. The excessive blossom lasts only a week and should therefore hardly be included in the description. *Prunus serrulata* 'Amanogawa' is an exception. As there is not a great choice of columnar forms, this type of tree sometimes actually has to be used because of its shape.

Shrubs   Barberry is a disaster as a hedge: when carrying out work under the hedge, the thorns penetrate even through gloves, whereupon the hands quickly become inflamed. The leaves of the holly also have sharp prickles.

This is why the smooth-edged 'Pyramidalis' variety is usually on the plant lists.

I do not like variegated shrubs either. Of the cherry-laurels, the variety most frequently grown, 'Rotundifolia', is the least attractive because of the incongruous pale colour of the foliage and the fact that it is sensitive to frost, especially in windy areas.

I do not use the following shrubs often: *Aucuba japonica* 'Variegata', *Berberis thunbergii* 'Atropurpurea', *Berberis vulgaris*, *Corylus avelana* 'Contorta', *Euonymus europaeus*, *Forsythia intermedia*, and *Prunus laurocerasus* 'Rotundifolia'.

Roses   Hybrid tea roses with large flowers are suitable for a dry climate. These roses are totally unsuitable for a rainy, chilly country such as the Netherlands: the flowers are weighted down. With some roses, the bud does not open in a wet spell. Many new Austin roses, which the grower himself called "English roses", have mixed colours, often pink and yellow or apricot.

The size of the blooms is not in proportion to that of the plant. Perhaps even the extremely popular red rose, 'Ena Harkness', is in my view unsuitable because the (excessively) large flowers are weighted down when it rains.

I do not see many opportunities to use standard roses, with the exception of weeping standard roses. I do not like very tender roses either.

Conifers Conifers are used only sparingly in the plans. In my opinion, *Chamaecyparis lawsoniana* and varieties, *Taxus media* 'Hicksii' and *Thuja occidentalis* are totally unsuitable for garden use. Cypresses are incongruous from the point of view of colour and also grow less well on damper ground. This yew tree looks flossy and disintegrates in later life. Its excessive production of berries can also actually be dangerous for children in the neighbourhood. The thuja mentioned turns a drab bronze colour in winter and also tends to disintegrate when used as hedging.

I do not like conifers with striking yellow and blue needles or scales, but they can sometimes be needed to create atmosphere.

Climbing plants Either a plant is pretty or it is not. The firethorn *(Pyracantha)* is indeed pretty, but despite this, I never plant it. If a certain plant can be seen in the gardens of both neighbours, I do not need to have one myself. And why do people still plant the eternal Russian vine or mile-a-minute? There is no need to use it for rapid growth: the wild old man's beard *(Clematis vitalba)*, which is indigenous to Europe, grows much faster, is more vigorous and has a more attractive structure. The Russian vine *(Polygonum aubertii)* looks exotic, but it is only very rarely appropriate.

In 1987, on my advice, Clematis montana was grown up the birch trees. The result is stunning.

Permanent plants Although I use permanent plants sparingly on the whole, there are some which for various reasons I never use. As a rule, there are only a few "stunning plants" in my plans. Not every garden owner loves gardening. Many people, myself included, do not like dealing with permanent plants. Nor do I use frost-tender plants. Like the golden rod, many asters get mildew on the foliage during the autumn. Butterbur becomes very ugly before the summer is over, as does the *Ceratostigma*. The following are unsuitable in my opinion: *Aster* (high- and low-growing species), *Petasites* (butterbur), and *Solidago* (golden rod, the tall species).

Bulbous plants I do not like bulbous plants which have to be lifted each year because of the hard work involved. Tender bulbous and tuberous plants are just as bad. The summer bulbs are nowhere to be seen in my planting plans. I can also never whole heartedly recommend dahlias, gladioli, and tuberous begonias, but I know many of my opinions have changed over the course of time. Perhaps I will actually use these plants more again in the future. The following are labour-intensive bulbous and tuberous plants: *Hyacinthus*, *Muscari* (with the exception of *M. neglectum* and *M. latifolia*), *Ornithogalum umbellatum*, and *Tulipa* (with the exception of some botanical species).

Fruit plants Depending on the wishes of the garden owner, there must be some fruit plants in every garden. I want to make an exception for blackberry bushes with prickles, because cutting them back is one of the less pleasant jobs.

Annuals   Annuals or bedding plants do not appear in any of my planting plans, with the exception of those for the instant garden. They are too much a matter of personal taste. I do advise against putting too many different pots and pans on the terrace. It is better to use just one type of container or a single large pot filled with eye-catching annuals. This will result in a much greater effect. Annuals can be used as in-fillers in the first year after laying out the garden. In subsequent years, empty patches in herbaceous flower-beds can be avoided by filling them in with particular annuals.

I rarely use Lysichiton americanum *(left) because of its sensitivity to frost.* Muscari latifolium *is one of the few grape hyacinths whose foliage is not objectionable.*

Plant sizes   The taller the tree, the longer the period for which it ceases to grow. Only after several years, when the roots have recovered, will the tree

Trees   get back its former full crown. Local authorities and similar bodies are easily persuaded to buy large trees. It is my opinion that only a little time is gained by buying a larger tree. A smaller tree will take root more quickly and will therefore continue to grow. The smaller tree which is planted straight into the ground will catch up with a larger transplanted one of the same kind in a couple of years. To my mind, the gain in time is certainly not worth the money, particularly considering the extra risk that the tree will not take root at all.

Ordinary standard trees have a plant size (circumference) which, depending on the price, is between 10 and 18cm (4 and 7in). A single tree for a particular spot in the garden may be much more expensive and for such a tree you may work on the basis of the largest nursery sizes. A trunk circumference of 40cm (16in) is the absolute maximum. Large sizes of slow-growing trees are of course more expensive than large sizes of fast-growing trees. Even so, for a small garden, it is better to choose a slow-growing tree. If you want a large-sized tree there, it means that you will really have to plant a mature tree. For me, this is one reason for looking for a more columnar tree for such places. The following can be considered: *Carpinus betulus* 'Fastigiata' (in clipped form), *Fraxinus excelsior* 'Obelisk', *Quercus robur* 'Fastigiata', and possibly *Prunus serrulata* 'Amanogawa'.

Shrubs and hedge plants

In a new garden, people often want large shrubs. These shrubs actually grow so fast that, after a few years, the bareness of the initial stage is quickly forgotten. If they are on the outer boundary, hedge plants must provide privacy immediately. For this reason, the plants must be of a reasonable size. If the hedges in question are used in the garden itself and do not have to provide privacy, the plants can of course be smaller. Often large quantities of hedge plants are necessary. A small difference in price on a lot of plants of one type will soon have an effect on the total budget. With box and yew hedging, small sizes are also preferable, as they can then be looked after well from a young age. It is true that they are known for being slow-growing, but in good soil and if well manured, they actually grow quite quickly.

Clipped columnar trees which are reflected in the water. The trees provide little shade, but give form to a particular section of the garden (design 1991).

The garden designs

This chapter discusses some aspects that play a role when laying out a new garden or remodelling an existing one, for example the cost and the maintenance involved with each type of garden.

The majority of the garden designs shown in the following chapters illustrate remodelling of existing gardens rather than plans for newly laid-out ones. That is logical as the average person moves house once every seven years and usually not to a new house. If the cost of building a new house proves to be exorbitant, great savings are often made when laying out the new garden and, after only a few years, work is started once again on the garden. The faults in the first design then also crop up again.

What is more, as a rule people have much more spare cash for the second design. There are often old trees in existing gardens which are being remodelled. Care is also required here. It can actually be the case that a certain tree stands precisely in a future vista. It is my opinion that for the design of a garden, it is sometimes permissible to fell a tree. Trees should *never* be felled to obtain more light in the garden (or in the house). Trees also constitute part of the decision not to buy a property. A lot of shade in the garden does not have to be a problem; shade-loving plants can be used. Where thinning out is necessary, a larger tree can of course occasionally be felled to give other trees a better chance.

Cost   The costs of having a garden designed or remodelled relate to the materials and laying-out work carried out by professional gardeners. Typically, the total cost for a garden can be broken down as follows:

A construction which reflects the ridges of the house. Initially, it will look far too high, but when it is fully covered, it will appear much lower.

This design has many features from Art Nouveau:
various geometric shapes are used together.
The transverse axis is also typical. The amount of
paving, steps and ponds make the cost of materials
higher in this case (design 1995).

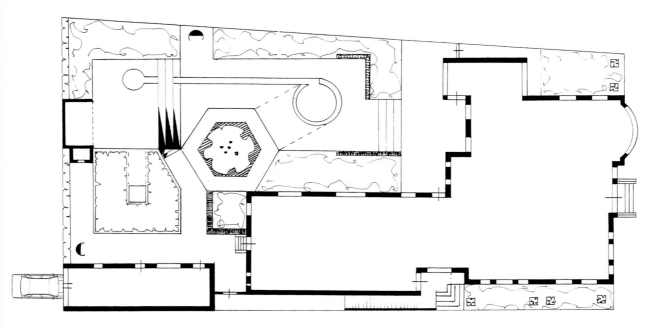

40 per cent labour costs, 40 per cent cost of materials, 10 per cent groundwork (and soil improvement) costs, 10 per cent planting costs. These costs are notional: the starting point is the cost of having the garden laid out by a gardener. If the owner does this himself and therefore does not spend any money on a gardener, the cost of the plants in relation to the total work of laying-out the garden is higher than the stated 10 per cent. In some of the gardens described in this book, people undertook a lot of work themselves, in others only a minimal amount. Nevertheless, I still want to give a good idea of the break-down of the costs.

Time for maintenance   When weighing up all garden plans, the time taken up with maintenance is important. Time need not always be seen as a restriction, but people who are always going away on long holidays must not take on a meadow. If there is little time available for maintenance, there should be few permanent plants, but a lot of woody plants and naturalizing bulbs instead. Large flower-beds with rhododendrons are admittedly expensive to plant, but require little maintenance thereafter. If you yourself have little time for up keep, and the garden has to be maintained by a gardener, the costs of more expensive planting at the outset will be "recouped" after a few years as you will need to spend less on maintenance.

Dressing   I am always astounded that every farmer knows that manuring is necessary to obtain the required production and that the individual garden owner uses fertilizers so little for his garden. In the first few years, rapid growth is important. The fertilizers used in this initial stage are different from those which must be used when the garden is fully-grown. In the first case, the fertilizer must contain more nitrogen, in the latter more potash. In addition to this, you need to know the acidity of the soil in order to adapt the soil to enable acid-loving plants to thrive, for example. Slow-acting organic fertilizers are usually advisable - for one thing, they need to be spread only once a year in the spring. The risk of scorching the plants is minimal, even if the fertilizer is applied when it is sunny. They are also considerably more resistant to being leached away than chemical fertilizers. This fully offsets the higher price. The reduced leaching effect will also do less damage to ground and surface water and the soil.

Making compost ***and pest control***   Wherever possible, sites are created where compost can be made. Nothing can beat homemade compost. I have no faith in compost made from household waste by compost-manufacturing businesses. How am I to attach any credence to certificates of cleanliness if the main constituents in the household waste come not from garden rubbish but from vegetable and fruit waste? Potato peel with shoot inhibitors, banana skins with poison, orange peel with colorants and

A cordon tree bed (left) and a Victorian flower-bed (right) brought a neglected landscape garden to life again (design 1989).

cabbage stalks with club root. Until the government bans most pesticides, this compost will continue to be a threat to your garden! It is not for nothing that some governments have set maximum quantities of compost to be used per square metre (square yard). There are no restrictions to the amount of homemade compost which can be used. Pests are controlled and plants protected. Nevertheless I prefer to talk about pesticides to discourage people from using them too liberally. The rather dangerous herbicide containing glyphosate as its active ingredient is described by one manufacturer as being less dangerous than baby shampoo. I do not have any objections to using them, but this comment actually leads to unrestricted and careless use. If you usually weed in dry weather, you often don't need these weed-killers at all!

Vegetable and herb garden at the end of a vista. When the plants have died back, the garden continues to be attractive due to the sundial and the green trees on both sides of the bench (design 1995).

Tools   The right tools for the right job – this is perhaps particularly the case with a garden. Just to go through the list quickly: spade, garden shovel, fork, rake, and hoe for the ground work and weeding; garden and lawn rake for tidying; hedge trimmer, secateurs, pruners, and pruning saw for pruning, and for watering a watering can and a garden hose with good accessibility to taps (faucets) are essential. Although I do not always keep to this myself, clean equipment is very important: a rusty or dirty spade is much heavier and harder to use than a clean one. With regard to pruning implements, spreading of disease also plays a role: it is desirable to disinfect them, but it is essential to keep them clean. It is of the utmost importance to keep tools sharp so as to be able to finish a job more quickly.

You cannot work with blunt tools: a whetstone used to be part of a gardener's standard equipment. A small electric grindstone is sure to recoup its cost. Sharp pruning equipment also leads to smaller cuts; a rough cut has a larger surface area, which increases the risk of infection from germs. Remember that left-handed pruners are also available.

Before you start... It is often my job to guide people through the garden plan. In so doing, I not only have to deal with the garden, but also with the garden owner. In fact, people usually want to lay out a garden themselves, but when it comes to the crunch, time often seems to be a forgotten factor. The gardener then has to take on more work, which will greatly increase the costs. Even in the initial stage of laying out a garden, people are thinking of the end result. A good target, but the soil can be brought up to scratch only if all fixtures such as steps, paths, ponds and so on are installed. If a pergola or arbour has to be made, the builders must still be able to walk over bare ground. I can well understand that if the garden has been made into a complete mess, there is the inclination to plant small plants and bulbs. *But this cannot be done* if the soil has not yet been brought up to exactly the

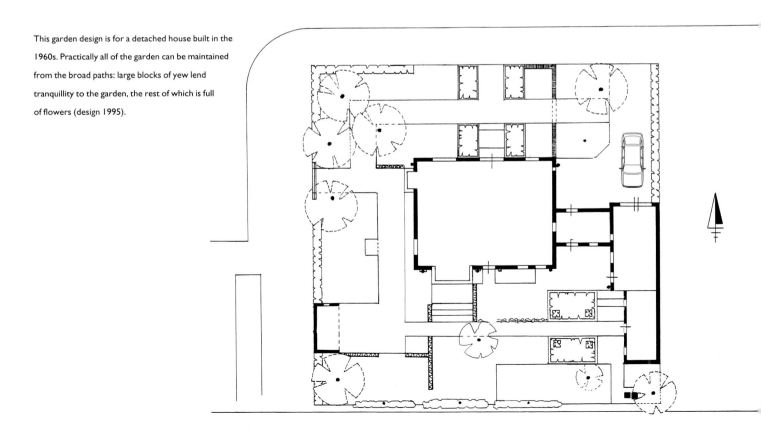

This garden design is for a detached house built in the 1960s. Practically all of the garden can be maintained from the broad paths: large blocks of yew lend tranquillity to the garden, the rest of which is full of flowers (design 1995).

This axis in the garden will look much narrower later when the plants have grown on both sides. The pillars with climbing plants will also help with this.

right level. If your garden is a heap of rubble, it is absolutely normal to go into a temporary depression: it is not pleasant always having to look at mess. Try to remember that, in comparison with the preliminary work, plants will be planted out in a trice once the mess is cleared away. With regard to plants, it is better to wait until all the non-living elements have been installed. Climbing plants, for example, often stand sadly around as they have no support to climb up.

The plants

Even with the best gardeners, I find that they sometimes spend too little time on plant work. The result of good plant work can be seen only after a year: has the plant flourished or has it merely survived?

Dig large, but not too deep holes for the plants and give them the necessary soil-improving materials and dressings. Always remove stones and rubbish. If there is netting around the compost in which the plants are potted, it must be removed. Nowadays, the netting is often made of some sort of acrylic material which does not decompose well. Remove the netting when the plant is in the plant hole, so that the roots are not damaged. Always slightly split the root soil balls of permanent plants which have come from pots so that they come into closer contact with the soil. Before putting the plant in the soil, the soil ball should also always be dipped into a bucket of water. After a year, you can see the difference between plants which were planted well and those which were planted badly – and the difference is great!

Although the plot boundaries are rather crooked, the lines in the garden itself are adapted to the lines of the house. The building always serves as a starting point. This plan shows how the irregular boundaries of the plot have been eliminated. House and garden now form a perfect unity (design 1994).

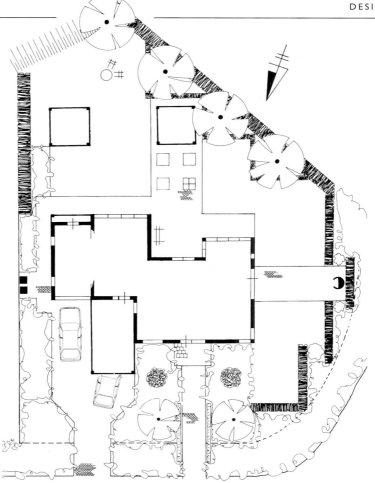

Lay-out management

Before you start laying out the garden, set aside a file in which to keep all the plans. The brochures relating to irrigation systems, paving materials, your favourite pictures from magazines, and the plant lists can also be kept in the file, so that you know exactly which plants you have ordered and which are still lacking. If subsequently, even many years later, you have to replace a plant, you can see from the old lists where you got the plant from. It is also a good idea to keep copies of the suppliers' invoices and the proof of purchase or guarantee for the pond pump in the file. You can then also see how much the entire lay-out actually cost you.

It is interesting to take photographs before work starts. Once the garden has been newly laid out, you will quickly forget how it looked before. Put a small bamboo cane in the ground at specific points so that you can take certain photographs from the same place. It is very surprising to be able to look at these side by side later.

Explanatory note to the plans

All my garden plans are consistent. It is essential to adapt the garden to the house. A circular bay-window can be repeated in the garden in the shape of a circular terrace or a round pond. A plot with a slanting edge can be straightened out visually, giving a three-dimensional effect. A cross shape can be found in most plans: the outer ends of the transverse axis then stretch to the outer ends of the garden and are often closed off with a hedge. The hedge is the narrowest form of dividing line, so that the garden continues to look spacious. The transverse axis is sometimes made by using water, sometimes by paving materials, and can also be a vista over a lawn with a statue or summer-house at the end. At the intersection, there is often a construction, usually made of metal, sometimes of timber, over which sometimes compact or sometimes free-flowing climbing plants grow. It can be seen from the photograph on the cover that even in a small garden (10x10m / 33x33ft), such a massive construction gives the garden an identity of its own. The constructions must be in keeping with the shape or the history of the house.

Lines and symbols   The paths in some of the plans are rather broad, even up to 2.5m (8ft). If the proportions are right on the plans, they will also be good in reality. Paths appear less broad if they are laid slightly more deeply. If plants are grown on both sides of the path, an axis is lengthened naturally. Black squares on the plans are waste containers. They constitute invariables in the garden plan, together with the path to the front door, the car, and if applicable the washing line.

Thicker lines on the plans represent constructions. A car is sometimes depicted on the parking places and entrances to differentiate them from other paved areas such as terraces.

Garden benches, chairs, summer-houses, constructions, and statues are essential to a design and are therefore always shown.

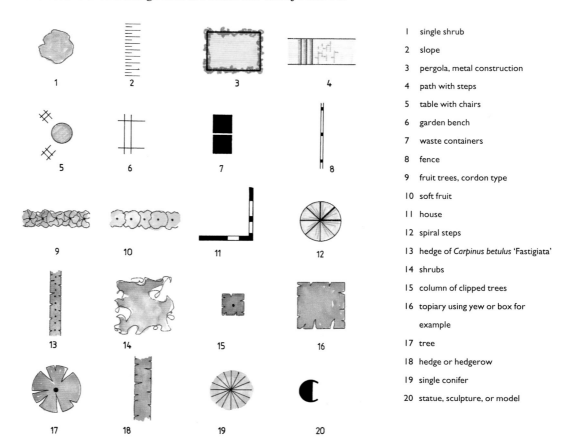

1	single shrub
2	slope
3	pergola, metal construction
4	path with steps
5	table with chairs
6	garden bench
7	waste containers
8	fence
9	fruit trees, cordon type
10	soft fruit
11	house
12	spiral steps
13	hedge of *Carpinus betulus* 'Fastigiata'
14	shrubs
15	column of clipped trees
16	topiary using yew or box for example
17	tree
18	hedge or hedgerow
19	single conifer
20	statue, sculpture, or model

Cables and Pipes In some countries a Cable and Pipes Information Centre is able to help if the position of existing electricity and telephone cables or water and gas pipes in a garden is not known. All cables and pipes are generally shown exactly on public utilities' plans, which can prevent a lot of damage when digging or when sinking posts. In Britain, you have to contact the public utilities companies themselves. Pipeline and cable detecting equipment is also available.

When a garden is being designed, the owner should, of course, be well advised of the position of any new cables and pipes for the water pump, the terrace lighting, and if applicable the air hose to provide the pond with extra oxygen.

The most recent trend is background sound for the garden: special weather-resistant cases in which speakers can be placed. I will have nothing to do with this, as to my mind there is nothing better than birdsong in the garden.

The construction is covered with ivy. If the ivy is closely tied, the shape will remain intact visually.

Town gardens

Town gardens are usually walled or built up on most sides. Not surprisingly, a different climate prevails in these gardens: the walls absorb warmth during the day and give off warmth during the night. A different planting scheme is therefore one of the options.

More tender plants can be used in town gardens. It is even possible to experiment with evergreen plants such as passion flower, *Jasminum beesianum* and *Clematis armandii* in an enclosed town garden. On the other hand, there are other plants which like to be in a sunny and airy site, factors which the town garden does not offer. Not surprisingly, such a garden is not suitable for roses and gooseberry bushes.

During the summer, these gardens are like greenhouses: the sun gives extra warmth there. In contrast, in winter the sun does not shine anywhere on the ground because of the high surrounding walls and the garden is a sort of cool box. Because of the lack of wind, tender plants can actually withstand this coolness better than the windswept conditions in a garden in the country. Town gardens can be seen as outdoor rooms and it must be possible to enjoy such an outdoor room from the house in winter too.

For this reason, many more evergreen plants must be planted here than in a country garden. As evergreen plants do not exactly flower profusely, this deficiency must be made up for by using long-flowering permanent plants. The slight hum of the traffic can be eliminated by the sound of flowing water. The tinkling sound of a waterfall or basin is clearer between walls. Because of the considerable maintenance required, no fountains and waterfalls appear in the garden plans shown below, but ponds do.

The type of soil in town gardens is often described as "urban soil".

It was possible to convert an old shed into an attractive veranda.

Over the centuries of occupation and garden alterations, the composition of the soil has varied greatly. Layers of rubble, oil tanks, and other rubbish in the soil have often disturbed the capillary action of the ground water. Rising air due to the warmth of the sun results in greater evaporation in the summer, despite the fact that there is very little wind. In a town garden, plants therefore have to be watered more often as a rule than in a garden in the country. Water the garden half an hour before you expect visitors: when the visitors arrive, the paths will then already have begun to dry, but the plants will still give off a lovely scent.

A typical problem when laying-out town gardens is the cats in the area, which immediately see the still bare earth as a clean litter tray. If you wish to stop other people's cats from doing their business in your garden, get a cat yourself.

Metal constructions are suspended above the garden. In this way, the climbing plants, which create a very lush impression, do not take up precious space.

The hanging garden in the town	design:	1986
	characteristics:	shady town garden
	soil type:	"urban soil"
	environment:	tall block of flats
	task:	enthusiast's garden
	restriction:	very overlooked
	details:	garden with deep shade
	lay-out:	own work; paving by a pavior

It is not possible to design a garden on the basis of a ground plan and photographs without going to see it for yourself. The ground water level and the extent to which the garden is overlooked by neighbouring houses can be seen from neither the plan nor the photographs. This is clearly illustrated by this garden, which is very overlooked. The difficult task of coming up with a creative solution to the problem of being overlooked from above was my responsibility. In this case, it is not the design of the ground plan, but the structures which rise up from it which play the most important part.

A small town garden should be arranged intensively: despite this, maintenance takes up only one hour a week. Given the small surface area, climbing plants are the obvious choice. With climbing plants, the extent to which neighbours can look in is reduced without too much sunlight being removed.

Lush plant growth surrounded by walls. Low sun does not reach the town garden, but this hardly limits the opportunities at all.

In this design, the use of suspended pergolas is striking: wires are attached to the wall from which a construction can be suspended above the garden in parts. This construction continues above the garden wall, restricting to a minimum the extent to which the garden is overlooked by a high block of flats behind. The advantage of this hanging structure is that there are no supports in the garden: there is still space on the ground, which makes the garden seem larger. Old dilapidated garden sheds are often broken up before I am called in to create a

design. I find that a pity, as often these small buildings can find a new use. The photograph shows how an old garden shed can be converted into an attractive veranda. Place old roofing tiles on top, remove part of the wall, and you have created another place to sit. In the veranda shown in the photograph on the cover of this book, a heating element has been installed on the ceiling: if the garden suddenly cools down in the evening, you simply turn on the heating as usual.

The comparatively widespread use of paving is offset here by the greenery on the suspended construction. The spacious lay-out gives the garden greater opportunities for use: meals can be enjoyed outside with friends and there are various little sitting areas. Variety is achieved in the paving by using wooden planks over large areas.

The planting scheme Climbing plants and large flower pots with hostas set the scene here. In a small garden such as this one, terraces are situated in as sunny a position as possible. This leaves only a site in deep shade for the permanent plants. Large cuckoo pint arum lilies are planted between the hostas. A cube of *Taxus baccata* creates a peaceful feature, which shows up the many types of permanent plants to better effect. In this garden, plants with edible fruits are actually in the majority: bilberry in the acid soil corner, grapes along part of the construction and Japanese wineberry along the garden wall.

View from the veranda. The yew tree section has taken seven years to reach its definitive shape.

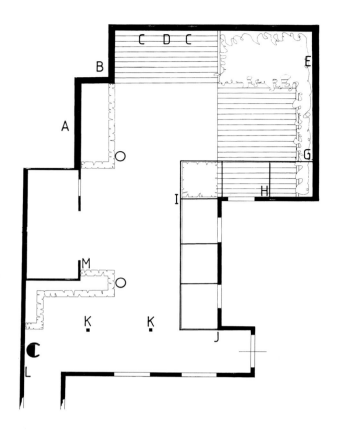

Climbing plants

A   Hedera helix (existing)

B   Aristolochia durior

C   Hydrangea anomala ssp. petiolaris

D   Akebia quinata

E   Clematis hybr. 'Jackmannii'

F   Solanum jasminoides

G   Clematis montana (existing)

H   Wisteria sinensis

I   Clematis alpina

J   Lonicera japonica 'Halliana'

K   Parthenocissus quinquefolia

L   Campsis radicans

M   Lonicera brownii 'Dropmore Scarlet'

Permanent plants

1   Lysimachia clethroides

2   Matteucia struthiopteris

3   Polygonatum multiflorum

4   Dodecatheon meadia

5   Anemone japonica

6   Brunnera macrophylla

7   Aruncus sylvestris

8   Aconitum napellus

9   Omphalodes verna

10   Pulsatilla vulgaris

11   Lamium maculatum

12   Primula vialii

13   Asarum europaeum

14   Astilbe sinensis 'Pumila'

15   Hosta sieboldiana

16   Cimicufuga simplex

Yellow corner

17   Helianthemum 'Golden Queen'

18   Viola 'Bullion'

19   Corydalis lutea

20   Helenium 'Butterpat'

21   Hemerocallis flava

22   Oenothera fruticosa

23   Waldsteinia ternata

The instant garden

design: 1994
characteristics: small square-shaped back garden
dimensions: 9x9m (30x30ft)
soil type: sand/peat, with mixed soil on top
environment: a lot of elderly people, not many pets
task: a quickly presentable garden
restriction: short-term rented property
lay-out: gardener

Laying out a garden for a rented property where the occupants are only there temporarily calls for big and above all cheap plants. These tenants want to be able to enjoy their garden immediately, as they will be moving house again within two years.

The garden had already been sown with grass and the ground was therefore already level. There was no trace of any design. In the corner there was a terrace made from aggregate pavers, with a couple of garden screens around it.

First of all, some structure was brought to the garden on the plan by using hedges as enclosures, and by using them en coulisse to make the garden look much bigger. Aggregate pavers are not in keeping with the period in which the house was built and the height of this paved area had to be altered. By turning the pavers over and lowering the terrace, this sitting area fits in better in the garden. The boring terrace,

This ground plan looks simple: the garden is obviously being thought of three-dimensionally. The climbing plants play the most important part. Constructions for climbing plants fixed to the wall offer great possibilities if there is little space for plants on the ground.

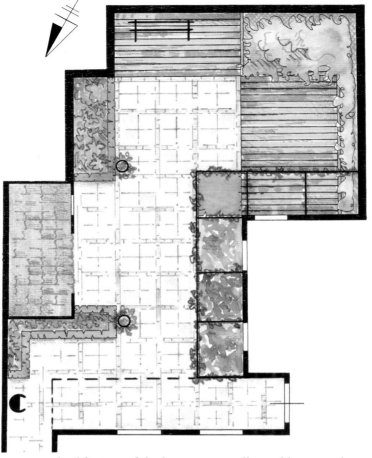

made as a standard feature of the house, was enlivened by removing a couple of paving stones from it and letting the hedge run on through it. By so doing, the terrace and garden now form a unity, which has an enlarging effect.

The planting scheme There cannot really be talk of a planting scheme here. All hedges are made using the Lombardy poplar (*Populus nigra* 'Italica'), which is cheap and which can be 2m (6ft) tall when bought. Some standard fruit trees complete the lay-out. Logically, the trees are right opposite the hedges, but also in a straight line in relation to the house. This gives rise to exciting vistas, which show up the garden furnishing to better effect. As a result of the diagonal hedging, the bottom terrace can still be seen from the living room (right below). The garden can be brightened up by planting annuals that can tolerate shade under the poplars. Fuchsias and impatiens spring to mind.

For creative people, the hedges could be made to "flower" by letting clematis grow up them and planting evergreen ground-cover plants beneath them.

The advantage of Lombardy poplars is that they can be planted out man-sized right from the start.

Maintenance Maintaining such an "instant garden" demands a great deal of pruning: the young poplars must be cut back to the main trunk each spring. But at the same time this is the charm of this type of hedging: small knots develop all over the trunk, just like with a pollard willow.

The older the poplars, the more beautiful they look. In this garden, there is also a lot of grass edging to be maintained. The advantage of a mature appearance at the start later becomes a disadvantage. This does not matter to these occupants, as they will soon being moving house again. Thus for them the advantages outweigh the disadvantages; they can enjoy the shelter and privacy immediately. And what is more the lay-out was quite cheap.

After a few years, once the knots have developed on the trees, enthusiasts can "graft" mistletoe *(Viscum album)* on to the trees. If berries are pressed into the hollows between the branches, there is the chance that they will spread and make the poplars evergreen in a way. Always press the berries into a hollow on the underside of a branch, so that birds cannot get at them.

The same garden a few months later.

Town garden		
with screens	design:	1991
	characteristics:	very enclosed garden
	dimensions:	8x8m (26x26ft)
	soil type:	improved "urban soil"
	environment:	tall 19th-century town houses
	task:	remodelling of garden
	restriction:	protection from being observed from the surgery
	lay-out:	gardener

A typical town garden surrounded by walls. A lot of paving is necessary to be able both to get bicycles to the shed via a door in the fence and to get from the back door of the house to the shed and the back exit. Despite this, no paths run through the garden: the paths are designed so as to act as a part of the terraces. This creates as tranquil scene.

An adjacent surgery presented more difficulties: patients looking in would impinge too much on privacy of the garden. In this case, the solution was found by erecting what is known as three-dimensional builder's wire mesh – transparent sections of galvanized wire mesh, through which climbing plants can grow. This also gives the garden some semi-enclosed corners, which increases excitement and makes the garden appear larger. In this way, three sitting areas were created. There is even a table permanently outside. The garden can be reached via spiral steps from the kitchen. The greater part of the garden is in shade, so that a flowery garden throughout was not a possibility, although the climbing plants do produce a reasonable number of flowers and thus amply compensate for the lack of colour at ground level.

In order to keep a design as cheap as possible, materials which are already there must be used. If railway sleepers (railroad ties) are retained in an old town garden, it does admittedly signify a concession on my part. However, I can console myself with the thought that, if

It can already clearly be seen from the plan that the depth increases visually as the plants grow closer together. The excitement increases if parts of the garden are not visible.

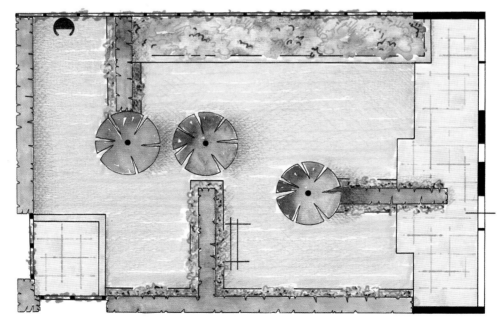

this were not the case, a great deal of energy would have to be put into more or less unnecessary transport to replace these materials.

The planting scheme

With regard to the planting scheme in this garden, I worked on the basis that a gardener would be maintaining the garden. Once a month maintenance requires a different approach to the one which is to be adopted if the garden owner carries out a couple of little jobs himself a couple of times a week. For this reason, it was decided in this case to use a lot of evergreen and permanent plants which are also good ground-cover plants, so that weeding is actually kept to a minimum.

The climbing plants need to be trimmed only once a year. Permanent plants such as *Bergenia*, *Geranium macrorrhizum*, *Smilacina*, *Symphitum grandiflorum*, and *Vinca minor* feature prominently. Climbing plants which predominate are *Aristolochia* and many botanical clematis such as *Clematis alpina* 'Frances Rives', *Clematis macropetala* 'Rosy O'Grady' and *Clematis viticella* 'Royal Velours'. Although the lady of this house wanted wild roses, to me this garden did not seem suitable for them. Only the mildewed roses which were already in the garden were retained. *Rosa* 'New Dawn' tolerates some shade well, so that it was possible to leave it standing.

The only way to make the garden really full of flowers is by adding rather special annuals, for example *Felicia*, *Nicotiana*, and *Verbena*, each year.

The view of the garden from above always presents a pretty picture of the previous design.

Although the garden looks fairly full, there are three sitting areas with permanent furniture. Thus a small party for fifteen people is not out of the question in this garden.

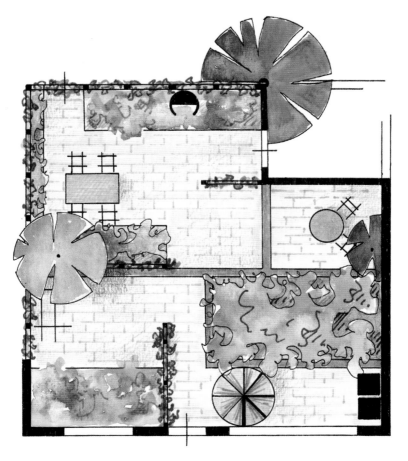

Town garden in the town centre

design:	1991
characteristics:	irregular-shaped enclosed garden
dimensions:	see plan
soil type:	"urban soil", mixed throughout
environment:	partly residential, partly business premises, old garden wall
task:	enthusiast's garden
restriction:	busy thoroughfare, owner's cats
lay-out:	gardener

The garden actually comprised two parts, one part of which cannot be seen from the house. The work began in an unusual way: the previous owner, who had lived in the house for twenty-five years, had put all the household waste out in the garden. If the waste had composted down, it would not have been such an enormous disaster, but in the layer of rubbish, which was more than one metre (3ft) deep (over the entire surface area of the garden!), there was also glass, metal, and plastic. It will thus be obvious that part of the costs were spent on clearing.

The two roughly square parts of the garden are also at different heights. To join the two parts, an extra square was created in the form of a metal construction. This construction, which can be partially seen from the house, makes it clear that a further section of the garden

Cats always cause problems in a newly laid-out town garden. One solution is to get one yourself. Your own cat will keep all the others at a distance.

lies behind it, although this section cannot be seen from the house. An additional advantage of this construction is that it creates privacy by preventing people from looking in from above. The cats had to stay indoors for a while immediately after the permanent plants had been put in. The fully grown garden does not bear such a close resemblance to a cat litter tray. The three sections of the garden are also at three different levels. Each level has been given a different character, which has given rise to great diversity in a small garden.

The planting scheme

Lush growth with an old-fashioned feel which is in keeping with the old surroundings. Even in the empty garden, the existing ivy on the old garden wall adjoining the neighbours already gave some atmosphere. The three sections of the garden are different due to their situation: one section is in the sun, the other two are in shade. Different atmospheres were created by adding garden peat to the soil in a shady section to make it suitable for acid-loving plants such as azaleas. "Old stone ruin" plants such as the Spanish bluebell *(Hyacinthoides)*, large-flowered snowdrop *(Galanthus elwesii)*, variegated Arum lily and large cuckoo pint *(Arum)*, meadow saffron *(Colchicum)*, and holewort *(Corydalis cava)* are suitable bulbous plants for an old town garden. As far as the permanent plants are concerned, mainly the old-fashioned sorts have been used: *Aruncus, Astrantia, Dodecatheon, Geum, Helleborus, Hosta, Mertensia,* and of course my favourite, *Saxifraga cortusifolia.*

64

Although roses do not thrive so well in town gardens, I have, on request, planted the pure single-flowered 'Dainty Bess' rose between the permanent plants which can be seen from the living room. This rose began to be cultivated at the beginning of the twentieth century and can be planted at random between the flowers.

The section in deep shade called for a special assortment: *Asarum europaeum*, *Geranium phaeum*, *Symphitum azureum*, *Tiarella*, *Veratrum album*, and ferns such as *Matteucia,* and *Polystichum Blechnum*.

The Lonicera japonica *'Halliana' growing up the construction gives greater depth to the garden.*

Maintenance

Maintenance consists of tying and pruning the climbing plants twice a year, trimming the holly *(Ilex aquifolium)* columns back into shape, and taking care of the great variety of permanent plants. The advantage of an town centre garden is that weed seeds are rarely blown in from outside. In such a full garden, weeds will hardly get a chance to "jockey" the other plants out of their position.

In summer, the garden will, of course, have to be watered now and again, particularly because of the large tree which takes a lot of water from the ground. It is an old wives' tale that the garden cannot be watered in sunshine during the day because the foliage would be scorched, as the drops were said to act as magnifying glasses. Take it from me: the water to put the fire out is already there on the foliage! So give the garden a good watering whenever it suits you.

The steps lead to the roof terrace from which the whole garden can be seen.

The different sections of the garden are   The steps indicate that there are

linked by a metal construction.   various differences in height.

Town garden,
two in one

design:	1980/1992	
characteristics:	18th- and 19th-century houses	
dimensions:	12x4m (40x13ft)	
soil type:	"urban soil"	
environment:	tall town houses dating from the beginning of the 20th century	
task:	to combine two gardens	
restriction:	deep shade from the tall surrounding houses	
lay-out:	own work	

This commission involved two small town gardens separated by a fence. If the occupants on both sides of the dividing line fall in love, the fence can of course be pulled down. Many years ago, I had created a design for one of the gardens. It was now my task to make a single entity of both gardens and in so doing to remove all trace of the earlier dividing line.

The fact that both gardens were on different levels presented a problem in this case. The difference in height would not be attractive in the combined garden. For this reason, part of the section which had previously been laid-out was also levelled to create a better sense of proportion between the low and the high section and to blur the old dividing line between the properties. No real trees can be planted in a small, shady town garden; but despite this, the garden must have some "height". This was provided by a construction for climbing plants to grow up. This gave the garden greater depth and a lusher appearance.

The cost of laying out such a small garden may seem high, due in part to the expense of hiring skips to remove waste and surplus soil. The costs also included a ready-formed glass fibre pond. The construction for climbing plants was made specially for this garden.

The planting scheme

The planting comprises espalier trees. Each year, the apricot tree produces buckets full of fruit. The taste is disappointing, but the fact that this small garden can provide enough jam to feed an army is in itself remarkable. To quite a large extent, the shrubs are evergreen, so that the garden still looks attractive from the house during the winter. The following climbing plants were used: various varieties of *Clematis*, *Hedera*, and *Wisteria*. The permanent plants around the pond tolerate shade: *Asarum europaeum*, *Astilbe*, *Aruncus*, and the groundcover plant *Tiarella*. To give the garden an old-fashioned feel, some yew cubes were planted. In the photograph, they have been clipped into cones: the lady-owner found this much more attractive. The result of the planting scheme is an old-fashioned atmosphere with a tropical lushness – ideal for an outdoor room.

By way of exception, the small paths are kept narrow here so as to leave space for the plants.

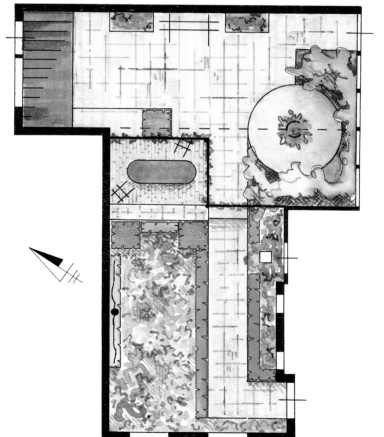

The dotted line shows the old property boundary between the two gardens. The owners gulped when the ready-formed pond arrived: such a pond looks much bigger above ground than when it has been installed in the ground. This ready-formed pond even had to be hoisted over the fence. A garden plan, and not the model in the garden centre showroom, thus indicates the true size.

Following pages: The clipped yews provide some tranquillity in the almost tropical lushness.

Roof gardens

The special climatic conditions on

a roof impose restrictions.

A combination of wind, full sun, and

a thin layer of soil are not conducive

to growing plants.

When designing a roof garden, before anybody asks me anything, I specifically stipulate that a fully automatic irrigation system be installed, because plants on the roof dry out quickly as the ratio between the quantity of evaporating foliage and the quantity of water in the thin layer of earth in a roof garden is not good. Also it is not usually much fun sitting on a roof: it is either too hot or you are practically blown away. But the view does you good. It is therefore my job to create a better climate for people and plants, so that the owner of a roof garden can also enjoy sitting outside.

A roof garden is a garden on a roof. Logical, you would think, but I do not call a roof on which flower containers have been placed a roof garden. A roof garden must give the impression that the roots grow in the roof and not in the plant containers on the roof.

A water computer is an over-precious word for partially automated irrigation. Partially, because, the system can be set up only at the moment in time and for the length of time when the garden has to be watered.
With a biting east wind, more water is needed, and less during a rainy spell, and this "computer" does not react to weather conditions. Even so, you can go on holiday with an easy mind if you know that a certain amount of water is being given each day.

The large plant containers made of zinc guarantee success. Even if the fuchsias are large, they have sufficient soil to prevent them drying out.

The town roof garden

design:	1991
task:	garden for living
environment:	terraced houses, beginning of 20th century
restriction:	roof is not designed to take any great weight
special circumstances:	also a children's play area
lay-out:	own work, assistance from joiner and welder

As wooden decking had been laid on this roof with a space of approximately 30cm (12in) between the planking and the roof, it was possible to sink the containers in the planking. Sections of chain link fencing were erected around the edge of the roof to make the garden safe for children. When the sections are covered with ivy, they will also act as wind-breaks. To make the roof become green quickly, a couple of fast-growing climbing plants were planted in the garden underneath: *Clematis montana*, *Clematis vitalba*, and *Aristolochia durior*. After only two years, these plants have already climbed up over two storeys and help to make the roof greener. Extra care must be given to make these plants grow quickly for a roof garden: at least half a cubic meter (half a cubic yard) of earth must be replaced with good, well-manured garden soil. This seems like a lot of work, but it will accelerate growth. It was possible to lay the pipes for the irrigation system under the planking. Small tubes run from the larger PVC pipes to the various

The roof does not want for a sandpit or slide. The fencing for the climbing plants also makes the roof safe for children. The colours on a sunny roof garden such as this one are cheerful and bright.

71

plant containers. The size and contents of the containers determined how many of these small tubes had to be used for each container.

The planting scheme

Trees in strong wind; the water computer ensures that they do not dry out.

There is not much choice of trees for a roof garden: they cannot be too tall and must be fully wind-resistant. In this case, the *Nothofagus antarctica* was chosen. This is a rugged tree which cuts across the stark lines of the lay-out straight away. In addition to the climbing plants planted in the garden below, the climbers on the roof will grow over the railings and will create a cosy atmosphere. There is even room for two apple trees on the roof. The railings on the roof are mainly covered with the Irish ivy *(Hedera hibernica)*, which is probably the least tender of ivies. In the autumn, birds are attracted by the berries of the *Parthenocissus quinquefolia*, which has to climb up the bars above the swing. Other horizontal bars are clothed in the Chinese wisteria *(Wisteria sinensis)*. Although *Wisteria floribunda* is prettier for a free-hanging situation, in this case it is too long before it flowers.

Nobody looks at a roof garden much in winter. In such a situation, evergreen permanent plants are not such a good idea. For this reason, flowering permanent plants which die back totally in the winter have been chosen.

A roof full of flowers in the summer is the result. To provide flowers in the early spring, the roof garden has been filled with bulbs, including

Iris reticulata, Crocus tommasinianus, Hyacinthoides hispanica, and *Narcissus triandus* 'Albus'.

A cosy roof-top *terrace*	design:	1993
	task:	garden for living, with flowers and fruits for picking
	special circumstances:	room to entertain guests
	lay-out:	own work

This "garden" is a mixture between a roof-top terrace and a roof garden. There are large flower containers on the roof, but as they are not sunken, and therefore remain visible, it cannot be described as a roof *garden*.

The proud owner does not need glasses to see his pears even in the first year after planting!

A small roof does not offer so many opportunities. This is why the balustrade is included in the garden. On the outer edge of the balustrade, a timber construction has been made. Flower containers fit into this construction. Ready-made plastic flower containers are always too small: as the plants grow it becomes apparent that a daily dose of water is not always enough. Even the water computer does not provide much of a solution to that problem. Sorry-looking plants would be the result. For this reason, I recommended that zinc flower containers be made, 20cm (8in) wide and deep.

A lot of sitting space is left on this roof-top terrace so that even fairly large numbers of guests can be entertained. Guests can even enjoy the home-grown fruits.

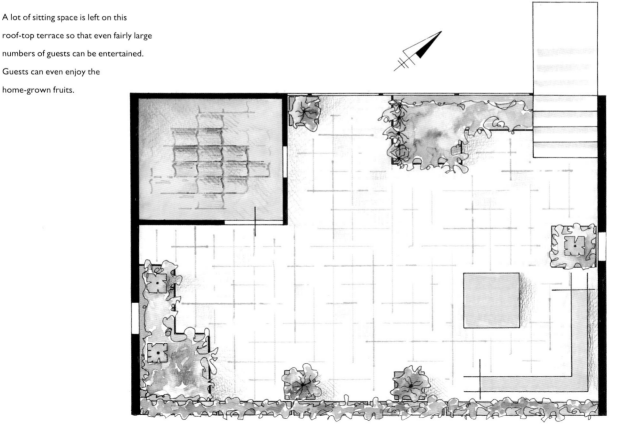

These give the plants enough room for their roots and will thus promote luxuriant growth. A sturdy construction is necessary to be able to take the very heavy flower containers. It is impractical to be dragging furniture out onto a small roof garden. It has therefore been decided in this case to use hardwood seats specially made for the terrace. To disguise the shame of using tropical timber, they have actually been painted! This practical "garden owner" built the lean-to himself, placing old roofing tiles on top which go with the eighteenth-century house.

The large flower containers are made from ordinary paving slabs which are bonded together using sand and cement mortar. If you want to join slabs together, never start drilling: the bit will get hot and in the worst scenario burn and the slabs will probably break. With good sand and cement mortar, on the other hand, you will be able to work wonders. It is important that the horizontal slabs are not bonded fast to each other so that there is and continues to be good drainage. It is apparent from this description that the ready-made materials from a garden centre, which are often expensive, are really not necessary. With a little ingenuity, you will be able to create a unique spot on Earth yourself.

The planting scheme In the first year, the *Clematis vitalba* should have grown 10m (33ft). Instead of which it still looks rather sad. A garden can give a lot of

Even in the first year after planting, the terrace looks full. In the future, the entire balustrade will also be covered with Clematis vitalba.

A window is highlighted by two Carpinus betulus *'Fastigiata' trees clipped into cylinders.*

satisfaction, but these little disappointments do happen too. It also goes to show that the garden designer cannot predict everything either.

For the fuchsias in the flower containers, the winter-hardy varieties were chosen, which do not have to be brought inside with the first ground frost. Precautions have to be taken only when a really frosty period threatens.

Cordon pear trees form a short hedge in a flower container. A white vine grows along a wire above the fence. A ground-covering evergreen blackberry bush trails over the edges of the flower containers. Even though it bears no resemblance to a vegetable garden, this roof-top terrace still provides a lot to eat.

The plant containers are partly filled with evergreen plants and partly with permanent plants. Behind the gnome – they like being outdoors – is Geranium macrorrhizum *'Spessart'.*

Terraced houses

The greatest problem presented by
terraced houses is that privacy has to
be created in a small space. In this
chapter, I shall discuss some designs
which guarantee privacy and which
make the garden seem larger.

The noise from neighbours which reaches the patio of a terraced
house can be annoying. One solution is a solid fence by the house or a
wall along the property boundary. Hedges quickly take up too much
room.

The fact that the gardens are often overlooked from the upstairs
rooms of the neighbouring houses also has to be taken into account.
For this reason, constructions with climbing plants are therefore often
used in the following plans. In general, the gardens are too small for a
stretch of lawn; in its place, more plants have been used, a lot of
permanent ground-cover plants and climbing plants in particular.
The gardens are often long and narrow, which always presents the
problem of deciding which visual effect should be selected: reducing
the depth a bit visually or actually greatly accentuating it by means of
a broad central path, for example.

As there are more of this type of garden, it seemed a good idea to me
to include the planting schemes in more detail in this chapter.

*The clipped yew on
a raised square is
tranquil to look at.*

Semi-detached	design:	1985
house, two under	dimensions:	6x6m (20x20ft) plus drive
one roof	soil type:	clay soil
	environment:	broad road with semi-detached houses
	restriction:	poor, wet soil
	lay-out:	own work

The former drive is now an attractive entrance, even in late autumn.

At first sight, it does not look as though much can be made of the small front garden, half of which is taken up by a drive. The garage had not been used for cars for a long time, but the drive was still there. It was therefore possible to make a garden out of this drive, which created an attractive entrance up to the front door.

It was decided to use small paving stones, laid upside down, so that the cutting edges face downwards. If low-growing plants are planted on the corner of a well-used path, children will be only too quick to use this spot as a short cut. For this reason, the inner curve was raised using grass-protecting pavers. A pyramid of clipped yew stands on this platform, forming a focal point in the garden. Ground-cover plants grow beneath the yew between the grass-protecting pavers. There is too little space in such a small garden for a broad hedge.

The hedges around this front garden are therefore made using the climbing hornbeam (*Carpinus betulus* 'Fastigiata'), a hedge which practically becomes a hallmark in the garden plans under discussion. A garden with many permanent plants looks dull in winter. Efforts have therefore been made to create a good sense of proportion between evergreen flowering plants and those which die back totally. This is a type of garden which is often found and for this reason I have attached a detailed planting list. The *Enkianthus* and the *Pieris* need garden peat; the other plants thrive in heavy and damp to wet clay soil.

The small garden is divided up by colour: this is the grey-white corner.

Following pages: The view from above really does reproduce the earlier plan.

77

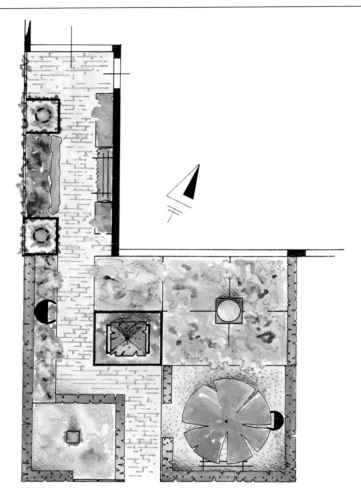

The drive goes along the garden. A large crystal ball is an appropriate ornament to stand on the square in front of the house window, so that the flowering plants which have been planted along the front wall can also be seen from the house. This also has the effect of enlarging the garden.

Semi-detached house		
	design:	1993
	characteristics:	long, narrow garden
	soil type:	clay soil topped with urban soil
	environment:	neighbourhood with a lot of children and cats
	task:	low-maintenance garden
	restriction:	occupants take long holidays
	details:	room to receive a large number of guests
	lay-out:	own work; paving by a pavior

People who go on holiday a lot and who also have a full-time job away from the house should not take on a lawn. This garden is rather narrow; the hedges on both sides therefore also have to be narrow to use the full breadth of the garden. In this case, it was decided to use the deciduous *Carpinus betulus* 'Fastigiata', the climbing hornbeam. The dividing line is partially formed by evergreen climbing plants. You cannot wander around in a small garden, so for this reason it was decided to lay a central path along the full length of the garden, with a square terracotta pot at the end, which is in just the right spot to create the perfect picture.

The terraces are large in relation to the garden. Planting columns on the corners gives the effect of reducing their size. *Carpinus betulus*

Tree

A   *Crataegus monogyna* 'Stricta'

Topiary

B   *Taxus baccata*

Hedges

C   *Carpinus betulus* 'Fastigiata'

Climbing plants

D   *Aristolochia durior*

E   *Wisteria sinensis*

F   *Hydrangea petiolaris*

G   *Euonymus fortunei* 'Vegatus'

H   *Rosa* 'Golden Showers'

Permanent plants

1   *Pulmonaria azurea*

2   *Lamium maculatum*

3   *Vinca minor*

4   *Veronica prostrata*

5   *Asarum europaeum*

6   *Epimedium niveum*

7   *Symphitum grandiflorum*

8   *Anemone japonica*

9   *Campanula poscharskyana*

10   *Helleborus virides*

11   *Astilbe sinensis* 'Pumila'

Permanent plants on platform

12   *Campanula portenschlageana*

13   *Tiarella wherryi*

14   *Waldsteinia ternata*

15   *Vinca minor* 'Gertrude Jekyll'

16   *Primula pulverulenta*

17   *Lavandula officinalis*

18   *Lysimachia clethroides*

19   *Dicentra spectabilis* 'Alba'

20   *Antennaria dioica*

21   *Stachys byzantinus*

22   *Smilacina racemosa*

23   *Aruncus dioicus*

Yellow corner

24   *Doronicum pardalianches*

25   *Solidago* 'Golden Dwarf'

26   *Trollius* 'Lemon Queen'

27   *Phlomis fruticosa*

Shrubs

I   *Enkianthus campanulatus*

J   *Pieris japonica*

K   *Salix helvetica*

L   *Rosa* 'The Fairy'

M   *Buxus sempervirens*

Bulbous plants

Iris reticulata 'Harmony'

Scilla sibirica

botanical yellow crocus

botanical blue crocus

Galanthus nivalis

'Fastigiata' was used once again for this purpose, but this time bought as a non-clipped tree.

There is a metal construction above the bottom terrace. Although the terraces are large, a small group of guests would not feel uncomfortable here. Small fruit trees have been planted *en coulisse* here to give the effect of lengthening the main path.

Garden designers are taught to plant large areas with only one species. This garden shows that in this case I go right against this advice: large areas of paving provide tranquillity and in addition one specimen per species has been planted of every possible small plant. In this way, the enthusiast gets the greatest possible variety on a small plot of land, but not at the expense of opportunities to use the garden.

I draw up in advance a list of plants which are in keeping with the atmosphere I have in mind. In this case, the large, tranquil areas of paving call for a counterpart: a very large assortment of colourful plants, which will later give an almost tropical lushness. Professional gardeners are not always happy with such plants lists, as it is time-consuming and not so lucrative to get only one specimen of so many plants from a nursery.

For this reason, I design a garden such as this one only for genuine enthusiasts who will also take some trouble themselves to collect the plants on the list. Deciding exactly where all the plants should be put requires much more time than the actual planting.

Even in the first summer after being laid out, this garden begins to get more depth.

The numbers on the drawing are not in order as the lists are drawn up beforehand. The numbers are then put on to the plan and attention is paid to which plants go well with each other. No plant may elbow out another; the plants for deep shade are placed on the north side of the shrubs and so on.

Planting bulbous plants has been calculated on the basis of ten or twelve small bulbs over an area the size of a saucer. Numbers are often based on the quantity which is supplied in a single packet.

An enclosed square garden

characteristics: terraced house
design: 1984
dimensions: 8x9m (26x30ft)
soil type: heavy clay soil
environment: looks out on a car park
task: garden for living
restriction: poor, heavy, wet soil
details: rented house
lay-out: own work; paving by a pavior

Failure after failure made the occupants eventually decide to take the garden in hand. The heavy clay soil did not let any water through. The water did not run away even under the house. New turf had twice

No matter how small the garden, there can be great variety.

This plan appears to produce great tranquillity. However, this tranquillity is misleading: when, after a few years, the plants have grown well, the garden will look luxuriant. A very large assortment of plants has therefore deliberately been used to achieve this.

Trees and hedges

A   2 *Amelanchier lamarckii* 'Ballerina'

B   4 *Carpinus betulus* 'Fastigiata' 2-2.5m (6-8ft)

C   7 'Conference' pear trees (cordon type)

D   4 'James Grieve', apple trees, old nursery standards

E   24 *Fagus sylvatica*

F   35 *Carpinus betulus* 'Fastigiata' 1-1.2m (3-4ft)

Climbing plants

I   1 *Akebia*

II   1 'New Dawn' climbing rose (already present)

III 2 *Lonicera japonica* 'Halliana'

IV idem

V   1 *Clematis alpina* 'Frances Rives'

Shrubs

a   1 *Aucuba japonica* 'Rozannie' (green, as the name suggests)

b   1 *Elaeagnus ebbingei*

c   1 *Ilex aquifolium* 'Argenteomarginata'

d   1 *Buxus sempervirens* 'Rotundifolia'

e   1 *Deutzia kalmiiflora*

f   1 *Weigela florida*

g   1 *Fuchsia magellanica* 'Riccartonii'

h   1 *Euonymus alata*

i   1 *Ligustrum lucidum*

j   1 *Mahonia japonica* 'Hivernant'

k   1 *Mahonia* x *media* 'Wintersun'

l   1 *Photinia* x *fraseri* 'Red Robin'

m 1 *Pieris japonica*

Permanent plants

1   *Asarum europaeum*

2   *Astilbe crispa* 'Perkeo'

3   *Brunnera macrophylla*

4   *Corydalis ochroleuca*

5   *Geum album* 'Leonard'

6   *Geranium macrorrhizum* 'Ingwerson'

7   *Geranium sylvaticum* 'Album'

8   *Acanthus hungaricus*

9   3 *Gunnera magellanica*

continued on page 84

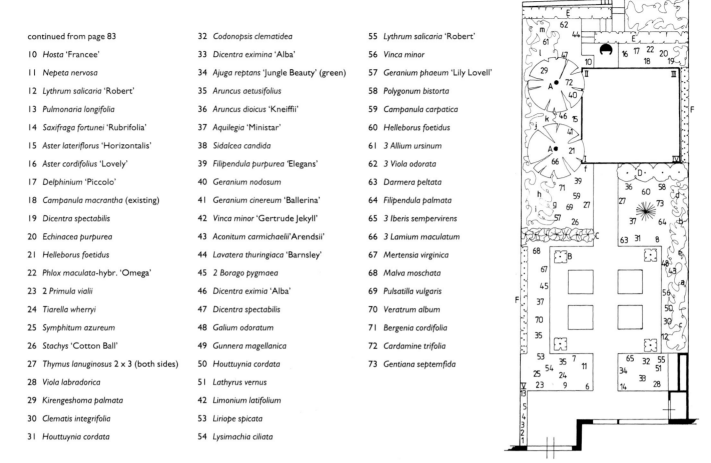

continued from page 83

10 *Hosta* 'Francee'	32 *Codonopsis clematidea*	55 *Lythrum salicaria* 'Robert'
11 *Nepeta nervosa*	33 *Dicentra eximina* 'Alba'	56 *Vinca minor*
12 *Lythrum salicaria* 'Robert'	34 *Ajuga reptans* 'Jungle Beauty' (green)	57 *Geranium phaeum* 'Lily Lovell'
13 *Pulmonaria longifolia*	35 *Aruncus aetusifolius*	58 *Polygonum bistorta*
14 *Saxifraga fortunei* 'Rubrifolia'	36 *Aruncus dioicus* 'Kneiffii'	59 *Campanula carpatica*
15 *Aster lateriflorus* 'Horizontalis'	37 *Aquilegia* 'Ministar'	60 *Helleborus foetidus*
16 *Aster cordifolius* 'Lovely'	38 *Sidalcea candida*	61 3 *Allium ursinum*
17 *Delphinium* 'Piccolo'	39 *Filipendula purpurea* 'Elegans'	62 3 *Viola odorata*
18 *Campanula macrantha* (existing)	40 *Geranium nodosum*	63 *Darmera peltata*
19 *Dicentra spectabilis*	41 *Geranium cinereum* 'Ballerina'	64 *Filipendula palmata*
20 *Echinacea purpurea*	42 *Vinca minor* 'Gertrude Jekyll'	65 3 *Iberis sempervirens*
21 *Helleborus foetidus*	43 *Aconitum carmichaelii* 'Arendsii'	66 3 *Lamium maculatum*
22 *Phlox maculata*-hybr. 'Omega'	44 *Lavatera thuringiaca* 'Barnsley'	67 *Mertensia virginica*
23 2 *Primula vialii*	45 2 *Borago pygmaea*	68 *Malva moschata*
24 *Tiarella wherryi*	46 *Dicentra eximia* 'Alba'	69 *Pulsatilla vulgaris*
25 *Symphitum azureum*	47 *Dicentra spectabilis*	70 *Veratrum album*
26 *Stachys* 'Cotton Ball'	48 *Galium odoratum*	71 *Bergenia cordifolia*
27 *Thymus lanuginosus* 2 x 3 (both sides)	49 *Gunnera magellanica*	72 *Cardamine trifolia*
28 *Viola labradorica*	50 *Houttuynia cordata*	73 *Gentiana septemfida*
29 *Kirengeshoma palmata*	51 *Lathyrus vernus*	
30 *Clematis integrifolia*	42 *Limonium latifolium*	
31 *Houttuynia cordata*	53 *Liriope spicata*	
	54 *Lysimachia ciliata*	

been laid, but the grass did not grow. Now that the garden had to be laid out afresh yet again, the structure could also be changed.

Drainage solved not only the problems in the garden, but also those in the house, Even the neighbours on either side of the house benefitted from it. Soil improvement made it easier to work the soil and plants were able to grow better.

Very high hedges stood on both sides of the little garden. As the garden was already rather dark, no trees could be added. Another solution to achieve height without standard trees was found by erecting tall metal screens and columns. The structures are more delicate when made of iron than when they are made of wood. Climbing plants now bring the necessary height to the garden. On the plan, the garden looks very austere, but the climbing plants really do make the garden livelier.

An area of evergreen plants had to be made at the bottom of the garden because of a car park at the back of the house. The view over the path towards the car park also had to be shut off visually by means of a screen with (evergreen) climbing plants.

In larger gardens, a zig-zag or link would achieve the same effect. To bring greater balance into the garden, another screen was incorporated. The half-concealed corners add some excitement and have an enlarging effect.

The view in from the back entrance is obstructed by the diagonal screens which add interest to the view from the house. They also add the necessary height. Trees are not suitable for this small garden; they would create too much shade.

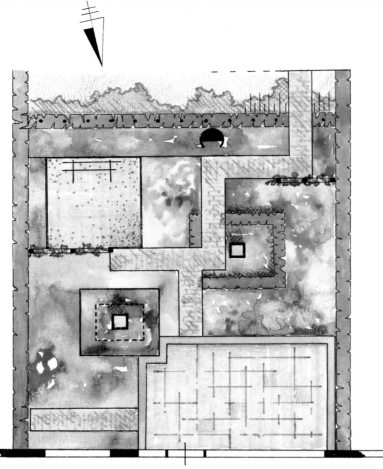

Once the soil had been dealt with, it was possible to add the permanent furnishings: ready-arched pilasters made of reinforced iron. Side wings were formed using tall screens with climbing plants: 7x7cm (3x3in) timber poles, to which reinforcing bars had been attached on both sides. This method of attaching makes the screens look more solid while they are still bare. Existing concrete slabs have been relaid, but this time with the underside uppermost.

The planting scheme

Although this case concerned a rather small garden, it was, despite this, still possible to create different atmospheres by way of the different corners. In the box square, there are only grey-leafed plants, to the right there is a yellow section and at the bottom of the garden there are only blue and purple flowers. A small garden which runs alongside the living room is seen more from indoors, especially in the winter: for this reason a lot of evergreen plants were an obvious choice. A number of the selected permanent plants also retain their leaves well in winter.

The neglected *thuja* hedges on both sides are now once again trimmed three times a year, which has made them look compact and tranquil. The *Lonicera japonica* 'Halliana', an evergreen form of honeysuckle, and the *Akebia quinata* were the main climbing plants used. The pilasters have been covered with *Lonicera henryi* and ivy (*Hedera helix*). A broad hedge of *Elaeagnus ebbingei*, a good evergreen shrub, has been planted on the other side.

Following page: Enjoying the garden from indoors. The garden can be enjoyed from the sitting room in summer and in winter.

Gardens for detached houses

With detached houses, the garden lies all around the house. This offers all sorts of opportunities to divide the garden up into different sections without losing any unity.

A vista runs from the kitchen door through the symmetrically laid-out vegetable and herb garden.

With these types of gardens, before starting on a design, I always first analyse which section of the garden will be used most, as a distinction has to be made between a garden which is to be solely for looking at and one which is for living in. A difference in atmosphere between the various sections arises spontaneously. This difference in atmosphere also arises due to the fact that one part of the garden often gets more sun than the rest. Lawns are used to allow shapes to stand out more and never to act as "infillers". Sometimes a lawn can reinforce a broad vista visually, but in a garden which has only squares, the lawn must also be this shape. Shapes on the outside of the house are repeated in the garden. This can be in topiary and sometimes in the shape of the paving or the shape of a pergola or other construction. Where the flowers can be seen from the house, I choose large-flowered plants at a greater distance from the house. The larger the paved areas, the larger the paving stones must be if the garden is to remain tranquil. The gardens of detached houses from the beginning of the twentieth century must be approached differently from the garden of a detached house dating from the 1950s. The history of the house therefore greatly influences the design. The use of flowering permanent plants has increased considerably and the expression "border" came into fashion in the twentieth century. After a hundred years of borders, I think that it is now once again time for something different. Permanent plants can also be used as edging, in flower-beds, on slopes, around ponds and

A broad axis runs from the living room towards a statue. The small, simple border is enclosed by a hedge which is planted en coulisse.

so on. Permanent plants look just as beautiful when used as bedding plants, as they do when used in a border.

Garden for a detached house in a spacious exclusive residential neighbourhood

design:	1990/1993
characteristics:	features from the 1970s
dimensions:	60x50m (200x160ft)
soil type:	sand on shallow layer of clay
environment:	neighbourhood dating from beginning of 1970s
task:	remodelling of garden
restriction:	a wet garden in places
details:	corner house very overlooked
lay-out:	own work, with Saturday help

The garden was laid out when the house was built. It was planted mainly with fast-growing plants to make the garden look green within a short space of time. The first step in remodelling the garden was to fell the poplars and to remove the elders *(Sambucus nigra)*. These were replaced by slow-growing and more evergreen shrubs. The design of the back garden had been made in keeping with the period in which the house was built using a lot of railway sleepers (railroad ties) laid diagonally. I have respected these shapes from the first design and have even highlighted them. The diagonals are most noticeable in the back garden. Although new vistas open up all around the house, each

There must always be a focal point at the end of a path. This makes the onlooker want to go into the garden.

A broad axis runs diagonally through the front garden.

The construction for ivy stands where the paths cross.

The broad main axis in the front garden cuts across a pond.

section of the garden still has its own shape and character: austerity in the front garden with the pergola being the ultimate static element; cosiness in the herb garden and landscape in the flower garden behind the house. The sombre, tall blocks of yew at the entrance give the house the status which goes with the situation. To accentuate the differences in atmosphere, the various sections of the garden on the four sides of the house have totally different planting schemes.

The front garden   The broad axis is flanked by lines of *Taxus baccata*. Large areas are filled with low-growing roses such as *Rosa* 'Immensee' and 'Repens Meidiland'. Another bed is filled with the lower-growing *Rosa wichuraiana*. Between the roses are some clumps of *Pennisetum alopecuroides*. The austere construction is covered with ivy, which must be closely tied back for the shape to remain clearly visible.

The side garden   An existing grove has been opened up to create the "secret garden". A heavy sheet of glass with a purple crystal ball on top has been installed in the middle of the small woodland garden with ferns. This contrasts splendidly with the natural surroundings. Woodcocks cover the ground in the opening to the grove. The garden should remain secret and for this reason there is not a photograph of it.

The back garden   The main axis in the back garden is made up of two lawns which are

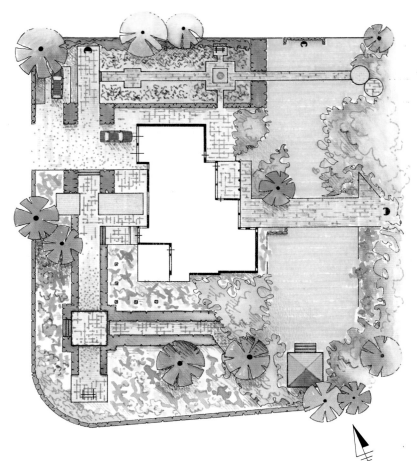

The different characters of the garden can already be seen in the designs. What cannot be seen from the plan is that the shapes of the roof have been incorporated in the garden three-dimensionally by means of the central construction. The different sections of the garden around the house are linked to each other by narrow vistas.

linked by a broad grass path. At one end there is a concrete plinth with a "coppa frutta" on top. The atmosphere around this fruit basket is created by lilies of the valley *(Convallaria)* and the yew tree, which is also dark green. The other end is formed by a flight of steps which leads to an oriental summer-house. In this way, the back garden is reminiscent of the nineteenth-century landscape style, in which oriental and Mediterranean elements often occurred. The present-day design is shaped by the diagonals from the 1960s. An oblique axis runs from the house to a small pond surrounded by many flowers.

The kitchen garden The cosy herb garden is in stark contrast with the other sections. The sun-dial, which was already there, has been given a central place in this formal garden. The garden bench is flanked by two upright spheres of *Ligustrum delavayanum*. Currants, raspberries, and herbs no longer grow scattered randomly around the garden, but form a garden of their own. This garden looks pleasant in winter too due to its austere shapes.

Detached house on a small plot

design:	1993
characteristics:	small garden around a detached house
dimensions:	33x14m (110x46ft)
soil type:	sand with peat
environment:	new residential neighbourhood with young families
task:	garden for living, with a lot of indigenous plants

restriction: lack of space
lay-out: gardener; paving by a pavior; constructions
             by a blacksmith

Left and right:
High constructions for
climbing plants were
required for the front
and back garden as
there was insufficient
space for trees.

The lack of space is a restriction here. This space is already partly taken up with the necessary evils: the car, the washing line, and the rubbish bins. The children must have room to play and the terraces must be screened off for privacy. A play area must always be situated so that the children can be watched from the terrace – not because the parents always find that necessary, but because otherwise the children won't want to play. In this case, the play area occupies a central position. To prevent the lawn from looking formal, a high metal construction has been built around it. The climbing plants will subsequently break up the straight lines. A similar construction has also been devised in the front garden, in this case because the presence of the car would otherwise have been too prominent. The local authority would not give permission to build a "pergola", which is what I call this construction, as it considers pergolas to be garden furnishings, which cannot be more than 2m (6ft) high. If the construction is called an "unfinished carport", it can be 2.70m (8ft 4in) high! That is probably the minimum height for a pergola, as otherwise many people would not be able to walk under it when the plants are fully grown.

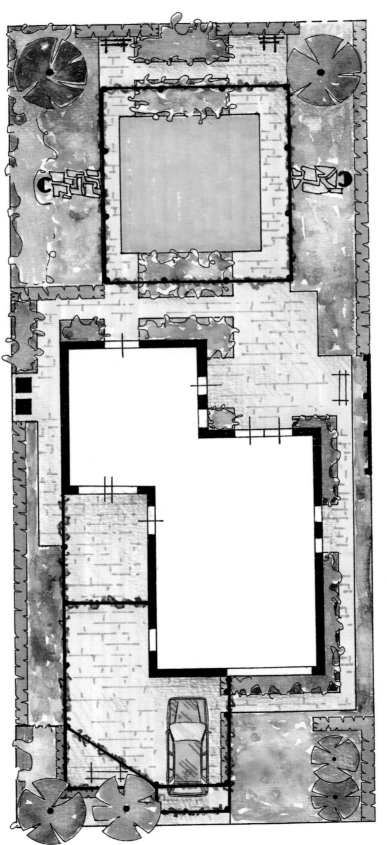

Although this is a small garden, the children's play area occupies a central position. The size of the floor plan of the house is not in proportion to the (too) small garden. For this reason, tall constructions have been installed in both the front and the back garden to compensate for this little minus point. Trees would result in too much shade in this garden.

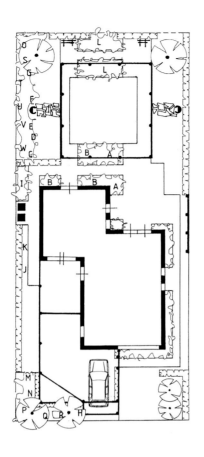

Low-growing shrubs

A 20 *Spiraea* 'Little Princess'

B 4 *Photinia fraseri*

C 1 *Weigelia florida*

D 1 *Exochorda racemosa* 'The Bride'

E 3 *Rosa nitida*

F 3 *Potentilla* 'Abbotswood'

G 3 *Escallonia* 'Donard Seedling'

H 3 *Vinca major*

I 5 *Euonymus fortunei* var *radicans*

J 5 *Hedera helix*

K 10 *Hypericum androsaemum*

L 20 *Lonicera nitida* 'Maigrün'

Tall-growing shrubs

M 1 *Mahonia media* 'Wintersun'

N 1 *Rosa californica* 'Plena'

O 1 *Carylus maxima* 'Purpurea'

P 2 *Euonymus alatus*

Q 2 *Ilex aquifolium* 'Pyramidalis'

R 1 *Syringa pinnatifolia*

S 1 *Ligustrum obtusifolium* var. regelianum

T 1 *Caragana arborescens*

U 1 *Sorbaria tomentosa* (or other species)

V 1 *Philadelphus* 'Lemoinei'

W 1 *Neillia* affinis

Working people do not like a lot of maintenance work: broad and above all a lot of paths make the work in the garden easier.

The planting scheme

It is desirable to plant evergreen plants around a small garden. Hedges are alternated with shrubs to give increased variety: *Thuja plicata* 'Atrovirens' and *Taxus* as hedging; *Elaeagnus ebbingei* 'Limelight' and *Prunus laurocerasus* 'Caucasica' as free-growing shrubs. A list of the shrubs used is given alongside the plan. With the exception of the *Sorbaria*, no fast-growing shrubs have been used. The lilac *(Syringa)* and mock orange *(Philadelphus)* are small.

Squares and cubes

design: 1984/1986
characteristics: enclosed on all sides by detached houses
dimensions: 30x22m (100x71ft)
soil type: heavy, wet clay
environment: small residential neighbourhood with a lot of green space
task: remodelling of garden
restriction: very wet, clay embankment
lay-out: own work; paving by a pavior

Sometimes things don't go as expected. The owner of the garden came to me to ask what he could plant on the spot where a full-grown cher-

This axis had been designed as a pond, but was actually laid as a gravel driveway. That does not bother me, so long as the lines still follow those of the design.

With hedges planted
en coulisse *the garden
actually looks longer,
not smaller.*

*The colour of the
veranda matches the
colour of the house.*

ry tree had been cut down. The outcome of this question was a new
garden, a freshly painted house, the interior of which was adapted to
be in keeping with the garden.

The modest house dating from the 1960s did not give much to go on.
All door and window frames were still painted brown. The soil type
could not have been worse: heavy clay on a layer of boulder clay,
through which the water could not run away. No wonder that the
existing garden had not been a success. Before laying out the garden,
drainage and soil improvement first had to be dealt with – a fair proportion of the budget was spent on that work. The embankment of
surplus soil at the rear of the garden had the effect of making the
garden look much smaller. By once again digging up one section of
the vista from the window, and by levelling the other sections, which
created a raised section in the garden, the embankment idea disappeared, and the garden looked much bigger. The precious soil from
the building plot could now be seen again for the first time. The back
garden looked sombre. The square flower-beds, each with a double-
flowered pink hawthorn, have been covered with pale-coloured
fine gravel to cheer this part of the garden up a bit. Shield ferns
(Polystichum) have been planted in the gravel.

**The planting
scheme**

To show the various squares to better advantage, the permanent
plants have been grouped by colour. Because of the stark lines, a great

A previous design can still be seen from
the plan: the paths and vistas are
narrower than is the case in most of
the other gardens in this book. Metal
screens and hedges planted *en coulisse*
make the garden look bigger. All axes
are directed towards the house, so that
in the winter the owners can also enjoy
the garden from the house.

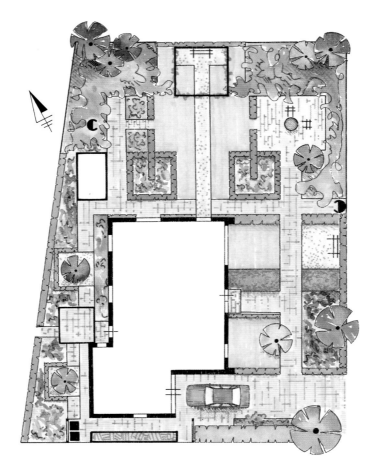

assortment of plants does not create a restless effect. It was therefore
possible to comply with the owners' passion for permanent plants.

An existing vine was trained along the underside of the gutter. In the
autumn, the bunches of grapes now hang in a row in front of the living
room window. Kiwi and a Virginia creeper *(Parthenocissus quinquefolia)* grow up the construction at the end of the central vista to
attract the birds. A square has been planted with low-growing pink
roses to lend tranquillity to the garden. The other beds contain an
almost infinite assortment of flowering plants.

Detached house	design:	1990
with spacious	characteristics:	enclosed section of the garden
back garden	area:	back garden 40x20m (130x65ft)
	soil type:	sandy soil on layer of boulder clay
	environment:	exclusive residential neighbourhood
	task:	enthusiast's garden
	restriction:	low maintenance
	lay-out:	gardener, plus a lot of own work

This is my first garden design with extremely broad paths. Although
the garden is not very big, I nevertheless got the idea of laying broad
paths. It was the desire to have a great assortment of flowering plants
which were accessible for maintenance which led me to this idea. A

square lawn interrupted by a path brings tranquillity to the back garden. The lawn is edged with low-growing pink roses. The garden is given an extra dimension by sinking the path by 20cm (8in). The main paths are almost 3m (10ft) wide: a neighbour was quick to call it the car racing track. As the plants grew, the correct proportions were created and there is no longer any talk of a racing track.

Where the broad paths cross, there is a metal construction which is as tall as it is wide. At first, the bare pergola looked far too tall; the correct proportions have now "grown in" thanks to the plants. Symmetry between the different sides provides the requisite tranquillity, which is also necessary as a great assortment of permanent plants has been used. The narrow hedges, which are at right angles to the windows of the house, have been planted *en coulisse*; they take away less of the view and provide increased depth. They also link the construction for climbing plants with the rest of the garden. There is still space left over for a compost heap and a vegetable garden. With a simple design, such as for this back garden, parts of the lawn can very easily be dug up later and replaced by a flower-bed of low-lying permanent plants combined with a lot of spring bulbs, for example. With a garden which is being established so slowly, it is good to assess whether there is sufficient time for maintenance. If that is not the case, the lawn can simply stay as lawn.

The depth increases as the hedges grow. Rosa longicuspis *grows over the construction.*

The plan shows that the broad paths are
in proportion with the medium-to-small
garden of a detached house. Immediately
after the garden has been laid out, there
is a sense of disproportion, but when the
plants have grown, the proportions
correspond.

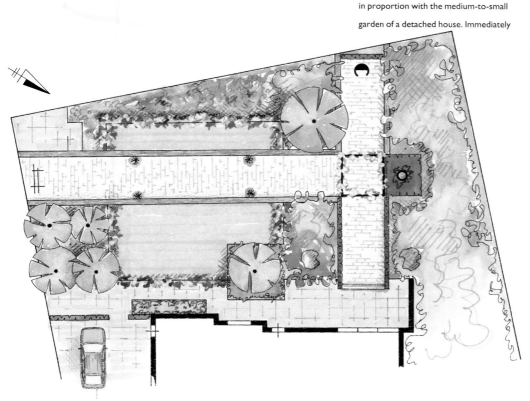

**The planting
scheme**

Two medium-sized trees have been planted: a *Liquidambar styraci-flua* and a *Gleditsia triacanthos* 'Sunburst'. The former was chosen for its magnificent autumn colours and the latter because of its splendid yellow, finely veined leaves, which give the large terrace a sunny feel. The hedges are *Carpinus betulus* 'Fastigiata', planted en *coulisse. Rosa* 'The Fairy' edges the lawn. The construction is covered with *Rosa wichuraiana*, a single, white, short-flowering rose which forms small rose-hips in the autumn. Contrast is created between the front and the back garden by planting the front one with large stretches of ground-cover plants and the back one with many different flowering permanent plants. Sadly, the experiment of planting the permanent plant *Darmera peltata* in the square bed beneath the *Gleditsia* tree was not successful: the plants could not withstand late ground frost.

In any estimate, there must be an entry for unforeseen expenses. The same applies with planting schemes: even if there are no thoughts of experimenting, disappointments can still be possible.

*Following page:
At the end of the
broad transverse axis,
the box has been
clipped into the shape
of steps which lead to
the garden vase.*

97

Garden with	design:	1991-1995	*The broad bridge*
different	characteristics:	enthusiast's garden	*suggests just one*
atmospheres	area:	front garden 35x20m (116x65ft), back garden	*pond now.*
		35x20m (116x65ft)	
	soil type:	sandy soil	
	environment:	exclusive residential neighbourhood	
	task:	remodelling of garden	
	details:	five year plan for laying out	
	lay-out:	own work; paving by a pavior	

A house which stands in the middle of a plot has a garden which is
equally important on all sides. All parts of it can be used for living. In
this case it is nice if each part is suffused with a different atmosphere.
Most gardens cannot be laid out in stages. In this case, it was possible
to use a space which had to be laid out last as a depositing ground for
materials. In the back garden, there was a small pond, which was not
in proportion with the size of this section of the garden. The pond was
retained as it was; a second pond has been "attached". By laying a
bridge over the boundary, the two ponds now look like one. It is also
convenient to use the small pond as a nursery pond for young fish.
By building a construction over the drive, the drive has become part
of the whole.
This entrance used to go along the garden. Old trees look best in a

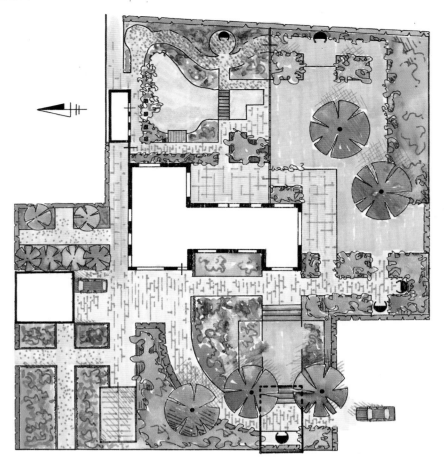

When remodelling a garden, the existing trees must be taken into account, especially if the previous occupier has planted many special trees. The existing small L-shaped pond formed the basis for the current larger pond. The planking disguises the fact that there are really two ponds. A vista from the house goes over the drive. This makes the drive appear to go *through* the garden and not *along* it.

Pillars of Carpinus betulus *'Fastigiata' break up the stiffness of the shed in the background.*

lawn. This was one reason for changing the shape, but not the position of the lawn.

The different sections of the garden are a sunken flower garden with banks in front of the living room windows, a vegetable and herb garden by the greenhouse, a small fruit garden with rhubarb plants, a water garden with shade-loving plants in the background, and a lawn with beds of shrubs and old trees.

The different sections run into each other smoothly, which means that new vistas constantly appear. The plan shows a few statues, but there could be many: in the middle of the sunken garden in front of the house, at the end of the axis in the vegetable garden, or even in the middle of the pond.

The planting scheme

The rhubarb garden was still included, even though the owner does not like rhubarb. The large leaves look so beautiful under the standard plum trees. A couple of trees have been omitted from the plan to show the line pattern more clearly. The shrubs in this garden are in a relatively shady site. *Symphoricarpos, Sorbaria, Ilex, Taxus, Ribes alpinum*, and *Rubus spectabilis* therefore had to be used.

Such a large garden is not suitable for small plants. Permanent plants with larger flowers can look very harmonious. Yellow-flowering plants should be avoided – *Kirengeshoma palmata* might just about be all right.

Country gardens

Some restrictions apply in the case of country gardens. The garden must be in keeping with the house in question, but also with the surrounding countryside. House and surroundings are linked by means of vistas opening outwards from the house or, alternatively, by having the house as their focal point.

In open countryside, the wind is stronger than within the shelter of a village. The wind factor is thus the greatest restriction to making such a garden inhabitable. Using fast-growing evergreen plants seems attractive, but is usually a disappointment. Nowadays, it also has to be borne in mind that the rural surroundings can change greatly within a short period of time. This also has repercussions on the choice of plants. As a rule, town dwellers are less affected by changes in the surroundings: everywhere is already built-up there.

The filled-in well has been built up again; the old brick paving is in keeping with the well.

Farmhouse garden

design:	1992
characteristics:	the property is a listed building
dimensions:	60x35m (200x116ft)
soil type:	sandy soil on boulder clay
surroundings:	village with farmhouses
task:	remodelling of garden, enthusiast's garden
restriction:	authenticity has to be borne in mind
lay-out:	own work, assisted by pavior

A farmhouse which is no longer used as such can be treated differently from one that still is. A distinction is therefore made between *farm gardens* and *farmhouse gardens*. The first term describes the traditional garden such as farmers used to have, and the second a garden round a farmhouse which now acts only as a dwelling place. The dif-

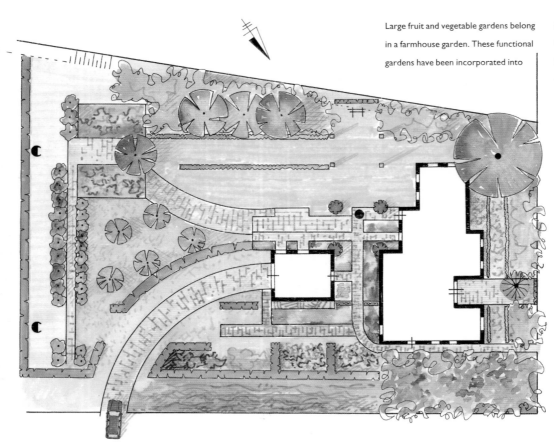

Large fruit and vegetable gardens belong in a farmhouse garden. These functional gardens have been incorporated into the garden here and they form a whole with the ornamental garden. The most important vistas are directed towards the 300-year-old lime tree by the house.

The large old lime tree (Tilia vulgaris) *has been given a key position in the new garden lay-out. The new shoots running from the base of the trunk will later be clipped into cylindrical shapes.*

ferent function of the property necessitates a different garden. But it is very important that the garden acquires a certain atmosphere, so that it is not evident from a great distance that the farmhouse is no longer used as such. The garden must therefore be simple. The vegetable garden has long occupied a central place in such a garden. There must be flowers for cutting around the vegetable garden. Different rules again apply for each area. Elegant borders in blocks of colour do not belong in the farm garden: the flowers should be large and bright. Some refinement can be brought to the multi-coloured flower-beds by putting fennel between the plants; these "gossamer-fine plants" soften the gaudy colours.

There is no place in a garden such as this for garden statuary. I prefer to recommend garden vases as ornaments. Other possible ornamental items are: a flax rack against a shed; a foot-scraper by the door; rhubarb forcing pots in the vegetable garden, or ordinary large plant pots. In the vegetable garden of this garden are two flower pots with *Poncirus trifoliata*, a plant which is reminiscent of a small orange tree, but which is more frost-resistant. A hen house need not be just plonked at the bottom of the garden. If it stands at the end of a vista, it will also attain ornamental value. Most farmhouses have a well and a washing trough with pump. A well should never be filled in and should always be reopened if it had been filled in earlier. The feeling of being able to use water from your own land is very special.

The planting scheme

As yew is poisonous, it must never be planted on a farm which is still in use . Cows will never again roam on this property and yew is therefore not a problem. Whole hedges of it have been planted. Some older plants have been cut back, so that they can later develop into spheres on the four corners of a vista. At the end of the transverse axis stands a holly hedge on two different levels as a backdrop for a garden bench. Just as with a transverse axis in the front garden, the focal point of the main axis in the back is a centuries-old lime tree. In this way the full height of the tree can be seen. Shrubs which block the view of the base of the trunk have therefore been removed. Old fruit trees can be used by letting various clematis plants grow up them. I have some difficulties with roses in fruit trees: the branches of the trained roses detract from the often magnificent old trunks of the apple and pear trees. At the bottom of the garden, a diagonal path goes between currant bushes to reappear at a spot with a bench. There are now seats at various places, so as to be able to relax and enjoy the garden once work is done.

Not the most appropriate furniture for a farmhouse garden, but concessions sometimes have to be made for comfort. I myself opt for an uncomfortable chair which looks good.

Detached house with open view to rear

design:	1993/1994
characteristics:	house dating from 1960s
dimensions:	back garden 20x22m (65x71ft);
	front garden 10x18m (33x59ft)
soil type:	sandy soil

A house half a kilometre (¹/₄ mile) away formed the basis for this design. It forms the focal point for a vista from the house. All the lines in the back garden were laid diagonally to this vista. A meadow situated behind the house continues right up to the garden. This suggests that the meadow belongs to the garden.

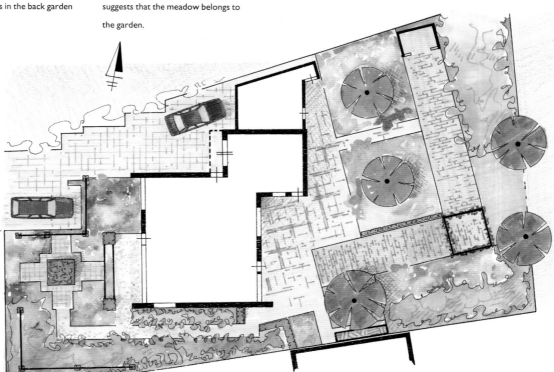

surroundings: farms, meadow to the rear
task: remodelling of garden, garden for living
lay-out: own work; paving by a pavior; welding work by a welder

Getting rid of the large lawn and laying a small lawn along the boundary with the meadow created the effect of enlarging the back garden, which is not very big. It now looks as if the meadow is part of the garden. In order also to include the house in the background in the garden, the main axis in the garden is directed at that house and the whole garden is made up of diagonals. The existing shrubs on the edges of the vista have been chopped down. The shady arbour (metal construction) gives the garden even greater depth.

The planting scheme

The occupants had definite ideas with regard to the planting scheme. They wanted blue, white, pink, and red flowers. Great store had been set by grey-leafed plants, but not by bronze-coloured foliage. They wanted to see yellow at most only in the spring and they wanted no purple. They wanted some plants which produce edible fruits and a lot of evergreen shrubs.

Practically right up by the house near the arbour, a hedge has been planted *en coulisse*. The view from the house is not restricted, which means that part of the garden cannot be seen from the summer-house.

This creates excitement and the parts which are visible acquire greater depth. *Davidia involucrata*, *Magnolia kobus*, and *Prunus avium* 'Plena' have been used for the trees. *Fuchsia magellanica* 'Riccartonii' has been planted in the permanent flower container in front of the house, flanked by *Taxus baccata*.

When the pillars have been covered, a transparent dividing line will be created between the parking place and the garden.

Evergreen shrubs used
Elaeagnus ebbingei; Escallonia 'Donard Seedling'; *Euonymus fortunei* 'Vegetus'; *Hedera helix* 'Arborescens'; *Ilex aquifolium* 'Pyramidalis'; *Ligustrum; Mahonia japonica* 'Hivernant'; *Photina x fraseri; Prunus laurocerasus* 'Caucasica'; *Rhododendron cataw-biense* 'Album'; *R.* 'Cunningham's White'; *R.* 'Pink Pearl'; *R.* 'Roseum Elegans'; *and Viburnum burkwoodii.*

Deciduous shrubs used
Deutzia x kalmiiflora; Euonymus alatus; Exochorda x macrantha 'The Bride'; *Fuchsia magellanica* 'Riccartonii'; *Hibiscus syriacus* 'Blue Bird'; *Kolkwitzia amabilis; Philadelphus microphyllus* 'Silberregen'; *Ribes* 'Jonkheer van Tets'; *Ribes* 'Rondom'; *Rubus spectabilis; Spiraea thunbergii; Syringa meyeri* 'Palibin'; *Viburnum bodnantense* 'Dawn'; *and Weigela* hybr. 'Rosabella'.

A grey-leafed bed was put in the central square in the back garden containing the following plants: *Anaphalis triplinervis, Anthemis cretica* var. *cupaniana, Artemisia schmidtiana* 'Nana', *Cerastium*

The colour of the summer-house is in keeping with the colour of the house.

tomentosum, Dicentra eximia 'Alba', *Gypsophilia* hybr. 'Rosen-schleier'; *Lamiastrum galeobdolon* 'Hermann's Pride', *Lavandula angustifolia, Perovskia atriplicifolia, Salix helvetica*; *Stachys byzantina* 'Cotton Ball', *Stachys byzantina* 'Lamb's Tongue'; and *Thymus serpyllum* var. *pseudolanuginosus.*

The broad axis is focused here on the houses in the distance. Even when the new plants have not yet been planted, the shapes already give some pleasure.

A country estate

design:	1991
characteristics:	manor-house restored in the 19th century, with moats and groves
dimensions:	500x500m (550x550yd) including moats and outer belt
soil type:	clay soil with organic matter from the moats
surroundings:	rural
task:	garden restoration
restriction:	in keeping with the building period
lay-out:	gardeners

A dovecote is not an item for the garden. Here it is situated in the outer grove.

This commission involved the grounds of a manor-house with an inner and outer moat with the belts of land in between. The grounds are famous for their "old stone ruin" plants: nowhere else does wild garlic *(Allium ursinum)* grow so profusely as here. These plants live thanks to the dredgings from the moats. The plants first had to endure the moats being dredged again, but later they will grow even more

profusely than before due to the fresh nutriments. Old raised sections have been left as they were. To get new vistas, new mounds have been raised. This creates a unity between the old and the new lay-out.

Old lime trees stand on the mounds, with the circles of shoots at their feet. It is true that on a mound surrounded by water, grazing sheep would appear to be the cheapest maintenance option, but then wire netting would have to be put up over a considerable length and the sheep would have to be fed, which is a lot of work, especially in winter. Mowing machines require no maintenance during the winter and ground-cover plants do not then need to be weeded. The wild-shoots of the lime trees would be eaten up by sheep. For this reason, the groves have been stocked entirely with ground-covering ivy.

Front view: the main axis, a moat in this case, runs towards the middle of the building, which was not customary in the 19th century.

The planting scheme

Bulbous plants go well in such a country estate, especially naturalizing bulbs which belong to the "old stone ruin" group of plants. In this case, it was decided to go for the cheaper species such as *Crocus tommasinianus*, *Hyacinthoides non-scripta*, and *Scilla sibirica*, which can be planted in their thousands to great effect. The shrubs in the following list also occur naturalized in old-stone-ruin settings. Shrubs which do not belong to the group, but which are still suitable, are the common lilac *(Syringa vulgaris)* and the guelder rose *(Viburnum opulus* 'Roseum'). *Parthenocissus quinquefolia* now trails over the walls of the moat. A fig *(Ficus carica)* has been planted alongside

An old lime tree has been transplanted to obtain a better vista onto the back garden.

107

Manor-house garden in landscape style: note the position of the statue on the far side of the moat.

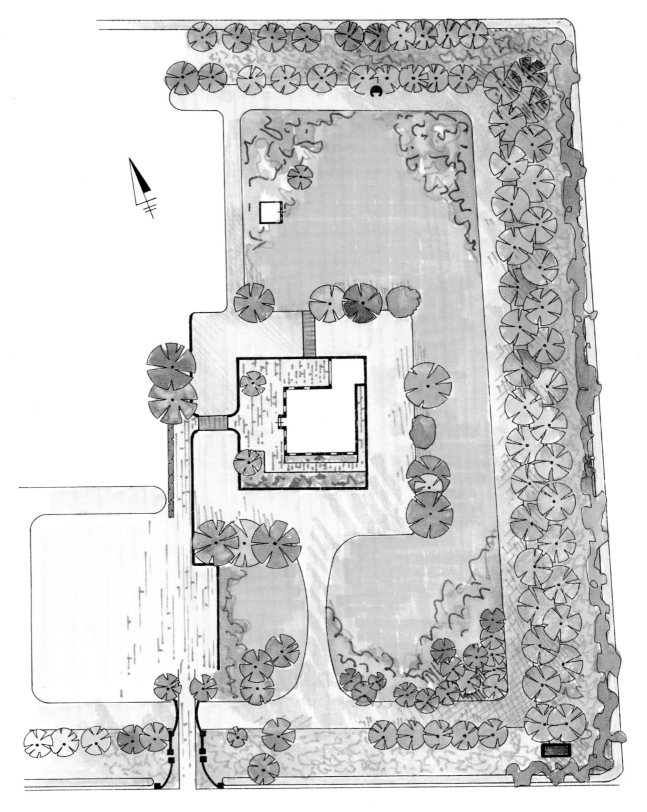

the summer-house. Banks have been planted with the ostrich feather or shuttlecock fern *(Matteucia struthiopteris)* and *Astilboides tabularis*, while the climbing hydrangea *(Hydrangea petiolaris)*, the white butterbur *(Petasites albus)*, and the dark-coloured mourning widow *(Geranium phaeum)* grow in even more shady sites. The last two belong to the group of "old stone ruin" plants, as do *Daphne mezereum* (mezereon), *Ilex aquifolium* (holly), *Ribes alpinum* (alpine flowering currant), *Rubus spectabilis* (ornamental bramble), and *Symphoricarpos albus* (snowberry).

The garden statue stands on the far side of the outer moat and thus extends the garden. I have still not discussed the colour of the bridge with the owner.

Detached house with modern architecture		
design:	1993/1994	
features:	view onto meadow	
dimensions:	35x25m (116x80ft)	
soil type:	peat on sand	
surroundings:	partially preserved old countryside in residential neighbourhood	
task:	varied, but low-maintenance garden	
restriction:	very overlooked	
lay-out:	gardener	

The austerity of the house was the determining factor for this design. The meadow with cattle lying behind the house has been made into a part of the garden. The occupants thus enjoy the cows more than the

The meadow behind the house is included in the design.

farmer who has to look after them. My first idea was to have a ha-ha to integrate the garden even more with the countryside. A ha-ha is a sunken wall which divides the meadow and the garden. The wall is not visible from the garden, and from the meadow it looks like a sort of dry ditch. As the garden had already had to be raised to be more in keeping with the house, there was a fairly big difference in height between the terrace and the meadow. Lowering this again slightly achieved the desired effect.

The practically blind south-facing wall of the house serves a purpose: it provides indirect light to show the works of art in the house to better effect. The large glass wall at the back of the house called for a terrace which was in proportion with it. It had to cover the full breadth of the house and the entire length of the garden. The width of the terrace is reflected in the width of the drive. To make this width visually attractive, some parts have been cut away along the rear of the house, where some fruit trees can be planted as part of the tree garden. Cypress oaks (*Quercus robur* 'Fastigiata') have been planted in the drive at regular intervals. A modern house demands modern materials: a lot of concrete and metal.

The planting scheme

In contrast with the great austerity of the house, there is a great assortment of plants. This has the effect of making the broad drive look narrower. The group of three trees to the right of the house is made up of

Despite the sparse plant growth, this garden has an atmosphere which is in keeping with the house (design 1993-1994).

This house dictates what should happen
with the garden: a modern design
demands a garden which is in keeping
with the architecture of the house as far

as form and materials are concerned.
In this case, the use of concrete and
metal is striking.

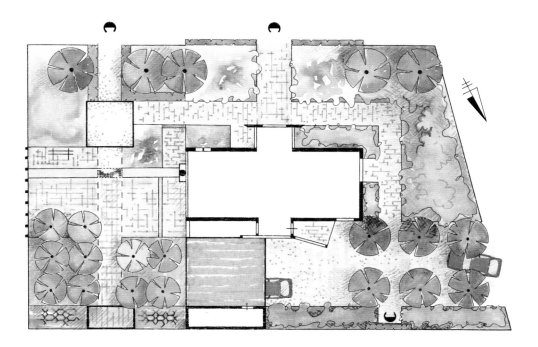

Turkish hazel *(Corylus colurna)*. As a continuation of this there are
two Japanese magnolias *(Magnolia kobus)*. The woody plants *Euonymus fortunei* 'Vegetus', *Juniperus horizontalis* 'Prostrata', *Rubus tri-
color*, and *Spiraea* 'Little Princess' have been used for ground-cover.
With regard to shrubs, I would also like to make particular mention of
bog myrtle *(Myrica gale)*, *Clerodendrum*, *Lespedeza thunbergii*, and
Sambucus ebulus, an elder which dies back in the autumn.

Simple, old,	design:	1991/1993
rural house	features:	small garden next to (own) meadow
	soil type:	sand on peat on boulder clay
	environment:	rural, old countryside
	task:	great diversity
	restriction:	very wet in places, goats
	lay-out:	own work, including the paving

A home has been made from a former almshouse. A grand garden
does not go with a modest house. There always used to be only country flowers and a simple privet or hawthorn hedge which enclosed the
vegetable garden with its beans and kale.
In this case, the choice had to be made between a rustic atmosphere
and a great assortment of flowers in order to comply with the owners'
wishes. An unsophisticated approach, with a vegetable garden and

simple hedges, has therefore been chosen for the area towards the open country, where the public footpath also goes. The back garden, which cannot be seen from the public footpath, was provided with a great assortment of plants, but still a simple design, so that there continued to be a good relation between house and garden.

Viewed from the house, the garden is straight, with various rectangles edged with box hedges right by the house, as is customary in an old farm garden. The paths should be narrow in such a garden. A central axis runs from this farm garden to a small veranda at the back. The old-brick path traverses a meadow. A transverse axis runs from this axis to a toad pond in more rural surroundings. A description of a toad pond is given in the next garden.

Right by the house, the form is classical. Provided there are also other forms elsewhere in the garden, this style, which is frequently, perhaps even excessively used, will not become dull.

The planting scheme

Fancy hedges are not in keeping with a simple house: yew and beech *(Fagus sylvatica)* do not therefore come into consideration. In this case, hawthorn and hornbeam *(Carpinus betulus)* were chosen. It was possible to use hedging types other than box in the back garden, which cannot be seen from the public footpath nor from the open country.

Where the garden is laid out in landscape style, plants which occur in the natural surroundings have been used. In places, Nature can even be left to her own devices: the bog myrtle *(Myrica gale)* can quite

112

A hawthorn (Crataegus) or hornbeam (Carpinus) hedge is more in keeping with a simple house than a yew (Taxus) or beech (Fagus) hedge.

happily spread vigorously on the wet sites. The long axis towards the veranda is flanked by *Alchemilla mollis* and *Geranium macror-rhizum* 'Spessart', among others; both are suitable for covering large areas.

Although it cannot be seen from a distance, there is a great assortment of trees, shrubs, and permanent plants in this garden. As red, yellow, and variegated-leafed plants are not used much, the overall effect does not, however, appear unduly sophisticated.

Low-lying permanent plants grow in large groups under the avenue of young lime trees. The lady's mantle (Alchemilla mollis) is the main eye-catcher.

House on the edge of open country

design:	1992
characteristics:	Scandinavian-style house
dimensions:	small garden next to large meadow
soil type:	peat on sand with boulder clay layer
environment:	last house in a row of detached houses
task:	ecological garden
restriction:	none
lay-out:	earth-moving company; gardener

An existing house had been renovated and extended, and in so doing a lot of red cedar had been used on the outside. The occupants had also bought an adjoining meadow.

In the new plan, the existing garden, which bordered the meadow, has been totally cleared, so that the old boundary has disappeared.

The front of the house adjoins the open countryside.

To forge house and garden into unity, the grass of the meadow has been extended up to the house. Even the little flower border right along the house had to disappear so as to create the impression that the house actually stands in the countryside. The trees used must be in keeping with that countryside, but close by the house, there can be a more sophisticated design. The indigenous, yet double-flowered bird cherry *Prunus padus* 'Pleniflorus' was chosen for this reason.

The surrounding countryside has also been taken into account in relation to the types of hedging: hawthorn and hornbeam. Hedging was required to give some privacy to the terrace and to camouflage the parked cars. There can now be said to be unity between house and meadow.

Reducing the richness of the soil

It was possible to remove the fencing around the meadow – cows will no longer roam there. In some places on the edge, groves have been planted with indigenous shrubs which tolerate wet conditions. This meadow is mown twice a year: in the first week of July and again in the late summer. It is never given fertilizer, so that over the years a meadow full of flowers will be created due to the soil becoming less rich. A toad pond has been dug in the meadow. This is a sort of large pond on a layer of boulder clay, so that it continues to hold water in both winter and summer. The banks on the south side are reasonably level. Frogs and toads can sunbathe there. On the north side, the bank

The woodland garden has gravelled pathways.

is steep, which creates variety along the bank, and different vegetation appears. The shrubbery alongside the meadow is chiefly made up of indigenous plants such as alder *(Alnus glutinosa)* and blackthorn *(Prunus spinosa)*, which tolerate damp conditions.

The garden from the living room.

House on the water

design:	1992
characteristics:	modern architecture
dimensions:	80x20m (260x65ft)
soil type:	peaty soil
surroundings:	scenic area
task:	enthusiast's garden
restriction:	very overlooked from public land, very high groundwater level
lay-out:	gardener; a lot of own work

With an elongated garden such as this one, there is the choice of whether this length should be visually reinforced or actually reduced so that the width is shown to greater advantage. In this case, the first option was chosen. All lines on the plan run along the full length of the garden: paths, dykes, walkways, and a pergola or arbour. Although it is narrow, this nevertheless makes the garden look big.
The high groundwater level presented me with major problems when designing this garden. Special and even common plants do not like

Following page: Galvanized poles give the garden a "second level" which matches the house (design 1992).

115

getting their feet wet. And as the occupants very much liked plants, it was desirable to have a great assortment of them. The solution was found to lie in erecting dykes, which are in keeping with the lake which this garden adjoins. The soil for the dykes came from the middle of the garden, which created a marsh there. A whole range of environments, from wet to dry, offers opportunities for a large variety of plants.

A lot of galvanized zinc has been used on this house. For this reason, zinc has also been used in the garden in the form of grille-metal walkways through the marsh. In this way, sophistication and nature are splendidly linked.

The planting scheme

Serious enthusiasts want a wide assortment of plants. The wet marsh section of the garden offers the greatest opportunities in this regard. I suggested making it into an iris garden. Irises stand proudly between the various marsh plants. There are a great many different, primarily Japanese, irises. But there are not so many gardens such as this one, with a more or less constant water level, which is perfect for marsh plants.

A wet garden is not suitable for most trees. They become dangerous in storms as their roots cannot go down deep. To reduce the risk of them

Sheets of grille-metal have been laid here to make it possible to walk across the marsh section of the garden. Metal sheeting topped with gravel prevents weeds growing through the metal grilles.

The garden is completely adapted to the extremely high water level. Dykes, ponds, and marsh form the basis of the design. Metal grilles provide the connection between the modern architecture with a lot of bare galvanized metal and the water garden. Their severe appearance is off-set by the scent of the roses which grow luxuriantly along the constructions.

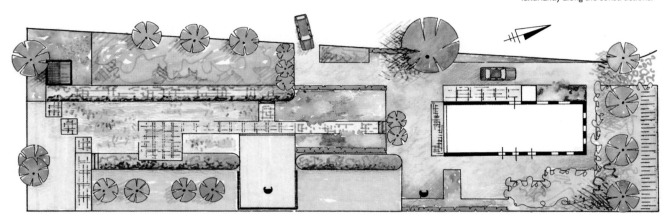

being blown down, only low-growing trees have been planted here: plantation planes and summer-house beeches. Pink, blue, purple, and white flowers grow along the main path under the pergola. The pergola is covered with pink and white roses. Some are long-flowering, others summer-flowering and yet more produce quantities of small hips in autumn. Large and small-flowered roses have been planted together. With the exception of the faintly scented 'New Dawn' rose, they all have a strong fragrance. To make for increased variety, various species of botanical clematis grow up through the roses.

This bronze statue, which fits in well in the marsh section, stands precisely in the main axis of the garden.

The following roses have been used: 'Adam', 'Blairi nr. 2', 'Blush Noisette', 'Climbing Iceberg', 'Dorothy Perkins', 'Félicité et Perpétué', 'The Garland', 'New Dawn', 'Pink Cloud', and 'Zéphirine Drouhin'.

Theme gardens

In this chapter I discuss a number of very

different gardens which

are characterized by a

particular theme, such as

a Japanese garden, a

patio garden, a pond gar-

den taking its inspiration from the 1920s,

and a rose garden, together with a planting

scheme for a greenhouse and a planting

scheme for a grave as a curiosity.

Japanese garden   A Japanese garden is usually not in keeping with other cultures and landscapes. Nor, as part of a garden, does it fit in well with other sections. The Japanese garden in question has for this reason been partitioned off from the rest of the garden by means of groves. In the second half of the nineteenth century, the Japanese garden was introduced into Europe, not always with success. Now that bamboo screens are imported from China, there are perhaps more opportunities to lay out a Japanese or Chinese garden. There are also nurseries now which specialize in the area of ornamental grasses and bamboo plants. It is amazing how well bamboo grows in more northerly climates. The good evergreen species in particular are practically essential for a number of situations.

In this case, it was decided to go for a Japanese effect as there was a lot of water around the garden and there were many differences in height. Such a garden is also in keeping historically, as the house was built in 1868. By laying slabs, it was possible to avoid a lot of groundwork. The problems of the existing differences in height could also have been overcome by laying steps, but this is much more expensive.
The slabs are made of concrete in this case, as I do not like using hardwood, not only from an environmental viewpoint, but also because timber can become very slippery in the garden, especially when it is in shade.

Simple pagoda with mossy stone. Japanese gardens are typical spring gardens, as it is then that the members of the rose family, such as cherry and hawthorn, flower.

Above left: the line structure is still clear in winter. The planks are at ground level in places; elsewhere they are one metre (3ft) above the ground. Moss growth can be accelerated by watering with rice water.

The slabs are made of moss-covered concrete. This method was chosen so as to prevent trees from being chopped down. Although the planting scheme is adapted to the Groningen landscape, shape and colour still manage to create a Japanese impression.

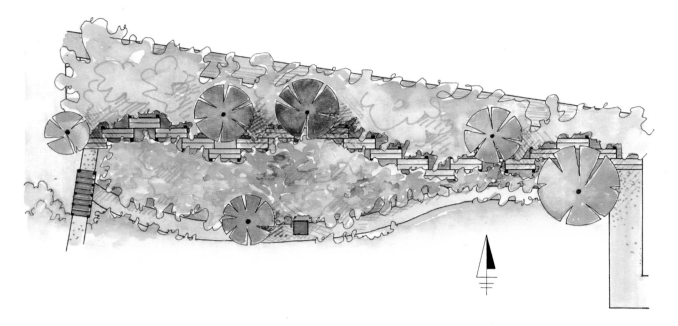

The planting scheme

Peaty soil is the perfect type of soil for a Japanese garden. This garden is on clay soil in full wind. It was therefore impossible to use the ideal plants for this type of garden. I had to use hawthorn, primula, and miscanthus grass instead of cherry, azalea, and maple. A bridge and pagoda, both painted bright red, also set the tone. Irises grow in the pond. Felled timber from other parts of the garden has been set down here, so that mosses can grow freely. One advantage of the slabs is that visitors cannot walk over the plants. This makes such a lay-out ideal for a garden belonging to owners who receive a lot of visitors: people can go right up to the plants without stepping on them.

I have made no attempt here to bring out deeper meanings – a Japanese garden designer is really needed to do that. To prevent a lack of harmony with the surroundings, no bamboo or stone lanterns have been used.

A patio garden　　design:　　　　1988

A patio is an indoor room outdoors. As a result of the surrounding walls, the temperature is higher. The walls also give protection from the wind. There are more possibilities for plants, but a patio is primarily a sitting room. Noise from outside is kept out by means of the waterfall which flows from the rose archway, which also serves as an alcove here. Supports for climbing plants made of white trellis clad-

The common hawthorn tree reinforces the Japanese effect (design 1990).

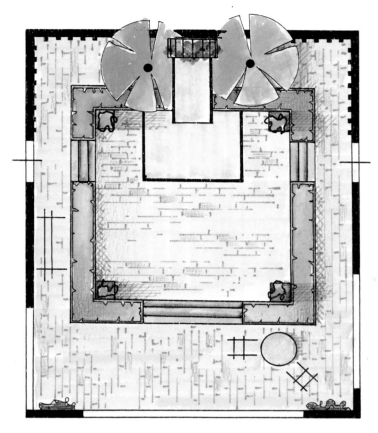

ding have been affixed to the back walls. Even without climbing plants, these brighten up the patio considerably.

The planting scheme

In a patio garden there is a relationship between the inside of the house and the garden. A garden which goes with a house that is starkly modern inside will be different from one which goes with an antique or classical interior. This patio has been conceived with the intention of installing designer furniture. For this reason, closely clipped box, trees pruned into spheres, a formal waterfall, and trained climbing plants have been chosen. The four (tall) pilasters have been covered with ivy. The intention is that the plants will be kept under tight control: protruding and swaying branches would make it into a romantic garden. Evergreen plants are also important: a patio garden with large glass walls between the house and garden must not look any less attractive in winter than it does in summer. In this case, the climbing plants have more vivid variegated foliage to make the walled garden less sombre. The planting scheme has deliberately been kept restrained: pots of tub plants can be put in as desired.

For the trees, standard *Ilex aquifolium* has been chosen, with *Taxus baccata* for the topiary, *Hedera helix* for the pilasters and the rose archway, and *Hedera colchica* 'Dentata Variegata', and *Euonymus fortunei* 'Variegatus' as climbing plants.

The stylish rose archways can also make good alcoves. A waterfall can cascade down from them or a statue can be installed in them. A mysterious effect is created if they are covered in ivy at the back.

121

Design for a pond

design: 1990
dimensions: see plan
lay-out: own work

When there is water in the pond, the axis will be reflected in it and will thus look longer.

The pond takes its inspiration from 1920s' architecture. It is formal and directed at the main axis of the garden. Originally, the edges would have been made of brick and the pond would have been made of concrete. Nowadays, because of high labour costs, a different method had to be found.

To create the formal feel of the pond, the edges must not be overgrown and there must be no water plants in the water. This would destroy the perimeter lines. An artificial pond had to be laid as the groundwater level was too low. To imply that the water level is natural, the pond lies low: the water surface is thus 60cm (24in) below ground level. Large concrete blocks have been laid under the middle of the pond: a statue can later be placed on them, even though the pond has been made from pond-liner. Putting garden statuary in the middle of the water is the best way to prevent it from being stolen. The reflection of the water also makes a statue look much bigger than when it is on the ground.

The pond now forms a perfect unity with the house.

The austere atmosphere is created by the galvanized grilles on the banks. Concrete girders have been laid under the pond-liner and the grilles rest on these. There is gravel between the grilles. To retain the

122

People can go all the way beside the water on the galvanized grille-metal walkways. Animals loathe these grilles and this prevents them from falling in the water.

reflecting effect, no plants can be grown in this pond. Duckweed must therefore always be removed. Even though no plants grow in the pond, the surface area is so large that there is enough oxygen for small fish. This pond is inhabited by at least a thousand minnows *(Phoxinus phoxinus)*, an indigenous, small, carp-like gold-coloured species of fish which multiplies extremely quickly. Bright red roses have been planted behind the pond, to double effect as they are reflected in the water.

The soil from the octagonal pond has been used to create a lozenge-shaped mound. One tip of this protrudes into the pond at one point. This gives a panoramic effect when viewed from above. For this reason, there are two garden benches here. The weeping willow *(Salix x sepulcralis* 'Tristis') trails in the water at this point and casts its shadow on the garden benches. Broad concrete steps lead towards the various vistas in the garden. The pond forms the centre. The main costs incurred in this case were for the pond-liner, the grille-metal walkways around the pond, and the concrete for the steps.

Concrete elements under the pond-liner provide support for the grille-metal walkways. The metal grilles thus lend a more austere air to the pond.

Greenhouse interior		
design:	1989	
dimensions:	6x12m (20x40ft), height 4m (13ft)	
soil type:	clay mixed with compost	
task:	atmospheric and useful	
restriction:	limited heating	
lay-out:	own work	

123

Pond in a 1920s' style. Austerity is created here by the galvanised metal grilles which can be used as walkways.

The pond is an integral part of the garden's longitudinal axis.

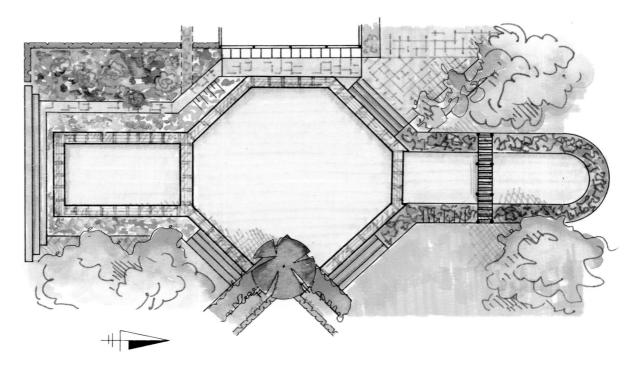

The position of a greenhouse in a garden is extremely important: the vistas and the incidence of light must be taken into account. A large pond in front of the greenhouse will provide more light in the greenhouse as a result of the reflection of the water. And from outside, the greenhouse will be reflected in the water from the garden, which will make it look bigger.

A larger greenhouse is like a garden. A plan for the structure of the lay-out is certainly just as important as the plants which will be put in it. The roof of the greenhouse will seem higher if some sunken areas are included in the greenhouse. This also increases the contents in cubic metres (yards), which creates a better climate. The difference between day- and night-time temperatures is less in a larger space. The humidity can also be affected by installing a pond in the greenhouse. In this case, the pond was installed at the lowest point so that it looks as though the water level is natural. The bottom of the pond is also insulated, so that the water reaches the air temperature more quickly. This means that lotus *(Nelumbo)* can be planted in it. A low-lying pond also makes it possible to install a waterfall, which further increases humidity. The circulation of the water also keeps it cleaner. Surrounding the sunken area with walls leads to an increase in the surface area which can take up heat during the day. The heat is then given off again to the air at night, which reduces the difference

between day- and night-time temperatures. The walls have been built using mortar with less portland cement and more lime. This promotes plant growth on the wall. Sheets of glass sheets have been placed on the walls to make the sunken section a bit more intimate. The main costs incurred were for the pond, water pump, and soil improvement.

Reflection from the water brings more light into the greenhouse.

The plants

To create a tropical atmosphere, plants must grow all over the greenhouse, not just on the ground and in the water, but also through the rafters. There must be a good ratio of evergreen and deciduous plants. When choosing plants, the winter temperature in the greenhouse is the determining factor. This greenhouse is heated only when there is frost, which means that the plants must be able to withstand a degree or two of frost. In an unheated greenhouse which is not insulated the soil freezes just as hard as outside. Nevertheless, tender plants can tolerate more frost in the shelter of a greenhouse than outside, as the biting east wind does not dry them out.

Climbing plants

It is not just the uprights of the supporting structure of the greenhouse which can act as support for climbing plants. There are numerous chains from the rafters to the ground to serve as plant supports. With the exception of the kiwi *(Actinidia),* all the climbing plants are evergreen. The rose will blossom very early in the year, although you will probably have to wait three years for it to flower.

Tropical luxuriance in spite of a low temperature.

125

The uprights are covered with ivy. There are many varieties of this climbing plant which would not survive outside, but which actually thrive well in a cold greenhouse. *Clematis armandii*, *Hedera helix varieties*, *Jasminum beesianum*, *Rhyncospermum jasminoides*, *Rosa banksiae* var. *banksiae*, and *Solanum jasminoides* grow in this greenhouse.

Opposite: Aluminium chains hang in the doorway to scare away birds, which would otherwise fly into the greenhouse.

Ground-cover plants

To create a lush appearance, all the ground must be covered with plants. The shelter of the greenhouse offers new possibilities. Mind your own business *(Soleirolia soleirolii)* spreads very quickly, as does the mossy *Selaginella kraussiana*. Both are available with green or yellow foliage. You can experiment with the colours to make patterns. Both plants can tolerate a few degrees of frost. The hard fern *(Blechnum spicant)* will grow well under the staging, where there is less light. *Acaena*, *Hedera helix*, *Selaginella kraussiana*, and *Soleirolia soleirolii* have been used as ground-cover plants.

Evergreen shrubs

To make the greenhouse attractive in winter too, evergreen shrubs, often of New Zealand origin, are everywhere. The climate of the southern island of New Zealand is reasonably similar to the climate in this relatively cold greenhouse. The following have been used here: *Camellia*; *Griselinia littoralis*; *Hebe*; *Ligustrum japonicum*; *Olearia haastii*; *Pittosporum species*; and *Viburnum tinus*.

Three years after being laid out. Phormium tenax 'Variegata' stands in the foreground in the sunken section.

The inside of a greenhouse is like a garden. A plan must first be made of the floor plan, showing the lay-out, water sections, ground levels, and so on. This guarantees optimal use of the greenhouse later.

Planting for a grave

design:	1988	
dimensions:	2x2m (6x6ft)	
soil type:	disturbed soil	
restriction:	must be laid out in summer	
lay-out:	gardener	

Choosing plants for a grave often has one restriction: the time of death does not always correspond with a suitable planting time. People do not like to wait too long when putting plants on a grave, but even so, it should be planted in the summer with plants which have been grown in a container. Unfortunately, this does not always happen, but this restriction can be taken into account when drawing up a plan. Rules are drawn up for each burial site and a grave must comply with them. Unfortunately, it is not always permitted to actually dig plants in on a grave.

On a grave site, the capillary action of the ground water has been disturbed: the plants used must therefore be able to withstand dry conditions.

It is almost impossible to make a good planting scheme on a grave if there are a lot of old trees at the burial site: shade and dry ground form a combination in which only a few plants can thrive.

For reasons of privacy, the photograph shown in this book is of a grave for which I did not design the planting scheme.

The planting scheme

Hedera helix and *Juniperus* 'Repandens' have been used for this grave planting scheme, with *Buxus sempervirens* 'Suffruticosa' and *Lonicera nitida* being used for the small hedges. A grave planting must be maintained regularly in the first few years, not only so that the plants stand beautifully by, but also to prevent them from drying out.

There must be a good ratio between evergreen and deciduous plants in a grave planting scheme. The flowering period can be extended somewhat by including the earliest flowering bulbous plants.

Design for a rose garden

design: 1994
dimensions: to be carried out to any scale
soil type: any soil which is not too damp
lay-out: for the constructions: a welding firm

This is a classic rose garden in a new guise. Each garden is different in shape and aspect. If note is then taken of the different periods in which the houses were built, it will be clear that off-the-peg garden designs cannot simply be applied to any garden. In this case, I want to show a rose garden which, with the necessary alterations, can be adapted to be quite suitable for most gardens.

This design can be used in an existing garden in the middle of a stretch of grass, but it can also be laid out in a small front garden.

The central path of the rose garden would then form the path to the front door.

The design can also be executed in squares. The pergola in the middle can then also be made square-shaped. If desired, additional rose archways can be situated on the lateral axes, which will give the unattached side flower-beds more depth.

This plan can be executed to any scale and for this reason it is suitable for both large and small gardens. A sunny spot is, of course, a requirement for roses. The paving depends on the site: in a small front garden, bricks are the best; in a large back garden, there can be probably be grass paths between the flower-beds. Clipping the edges is extra work in that case.

At the end of the nineteenth and the beginning of the twentieth century, a rose garden was meant to be lowered, similar to a "sunken garden". The use of flagstones as paving was then in fashion. (In a sunny site, flagstones do not become very slippery). The reverse is also a possibility: make the a raised bed. Steps will have to be laid in both cases. The problem of a lack or surplus of soil can be solved cheaply in this way.

The box hedges have deliberately not been planted symmetrically. But this does not disturb the balance. This planting method prevents the garden from appearing trite.

In a garden with formal shapes, climbing roses can be tied tight: in a romantic garden they can protrude freely and gracefully. This means that this design can be used in practically any garden style. Pergolas and rose archways are usually too low: a minimum height of 2.5m (7ft 8in) is desirable. Pergolas must be higher, namely 3m (10ft).

Water lilies in this pond would ruin the reflection of the Allotria roses.

I made this plan for general use in any garden. Plant quantities depend on the scale to which the plan is executed.

The choice of roses is extremely personal. One possibility is:

1 4 'Ballerina', height 1.8m (5ft 11in)
2 4 'Albéric Barbier'
3 'Repens Meidiland' with some 'Dainty Bess'
4 'Weisse Immensee'
5 'Swany'
6 'Pompon de Paris' with some 'White Wings'
7 'Stanwell Perpetual'
8 'Schneewitchen' (syn. 'Iceberg')

A *Buxus sempervirens* (6 per m² [yd²])
B *Lavandula* v (4 per m² [yd²])
C 4 *Carpinus betulus* 'Fastigiata'

Ontw. Studio voor Tuinconsult

The circular pergola can be made of metal. Galvanized water pipes are suitable for this purpose. If the owner is making the pergola himself, a square timber construction is easier. A splendid cube can be made using eight square poles 7cm (3in) in diameter. Standard lengths are 2.7m (8ft 9in) and 2.9m (9ft). Whether the construction is made of metal or timber, it is prettiest if painted in the colours of the house.

The planting scheme In a large garden, the box hedges are made using *Buxus sempervirens* 'Rotundifolia', while *Buxus sempervirens* 'Suffruticosa' is used in a small garden. Both lavender and catmint are available in high- and low-growing varieties. If the pergola is covered with roses which flower only once, I would recommend they be combined with clematis to achieve staggered flowering. Varieties of the *C. alpina*, *C. macropetala*, and *C. viticella* species are the most suitable for this purpose. In a small garden, weeping standard roses can be planted on both sides of the rose archway; in a large garden, these can be replaced by spreading acacias. The other axes end between columns of *Carpinus betulus* 'Fastigiata'. The columns can be bought when they have already reached a height of 3m (10ft). After two years of clipping, they will have attained their proper shape. Hybrid tea roses or floribunda roses in the flower-beds can be provided with underplanting. This does, however, mean that the roses cannot be earthed up.

General advice

I conclude here by examining factors which ensure that a garden succeeds or, on the contrary, fails pitifully. I also deal with a number of questions and requests which are often put to me.

Even in winter shapes still stand out well (design 1989).

The difference between success and failure

In relation to the subsequent years of enjoyment, the process of laying out a garden takes only a short time. For this reason, sufficient time should be spent on laying it out. Hasty work always leads to a poorer result. You should not rush things even if the planting season is coming to an end: the next planting season is only five months away! The garden can be filled with annuals for the time being. And what is more, the first summer can be used to get rid of the weeds. An amateurish approach can cause years of annoyance. For example, it is not easy to re-lay a pond which has been installed wrongly.

Of the many garden plans I make, some fail, for example due to cheaper materials being used than those stated in the plan. Laying the garden out inaccurately in the initial stage can have disastrous consequences. If a garden shed is not sited perpendicular to the house, it will always be an annoying element as it will look even more crooked if you look over the joints of the paving stones. Accurate work is the basis for a good garden lay-out.

Of course, plants can subsequently disguise some faults, but in winter, when the branches are bare again, a pergola which stands askew will once again look really crooked! Of course, some failures are down to me too: not asking enough questions about certain things can lead to a poorer result.

Happily, I am sometimes also very pleasantly surprised: the way some garden owners keep their gardens in perfect order, and likewise their

great ingenuity, sometimes result in such beautiful gardens that I can hardly believe that it was I who designed the garden in the first place.

Unsuccessful planting schemes

An adviser does his best to make the right choice for a particular site. But unfortunately the plan has usually been muddled up even after only a year by the garden owner. Well-meaning guests always bring a plant for the garden. Even worse are the acquaintances who see a chance to relieve themselves in the garden.

The worst, however, are the nurserymen and garden centres who resolutely provide replacements so as not to miss out on business. It is sad to see a 2m (6ft) high *Lythrum salicaria* planted by a small pond instead of the stipulated *Lythrum salicaria* 'Robert' which is 80cm (32in) high. *Stephanandra incisa* is usually replaced by *S.i.* 'Crispa', a smaller shrub with very unhealthy-looking foliage. The same is true of *Ilex crenata*, which is not cultivated much. It is therefore often replaced by the ugly *I.c.* 'Convexa'. The worst case in my experience is the client who inadvertently planted a 3m (10ft) high and wide *Gunnera tinctoria* in his small garden instead of the stipulated ground-covering *Gunnera magellanica* which is 15cm (6in) high! After all, the plants are the same height when bought. I do not know how often *Taxus media* 'Hicksii' has been planted instead of *Taxus baccata*. First let me give you some advice about letting a nurseryman persuade you to change your mind when buying: the first yew mentioned is

When visiting a garden for which a design had been made two years previously, it was a great surprise to see how much the depth had increased now that the plants were fully grown! (design 1991)

133

grown more because it is easier for many growers to take cuttings rather than growing from seed. They are therefore cheaper. It can be seen from this that nurserymen are not good advisers: different knowledge is needed for cultivating quality plants to that required for using the plants.

I have mentioned here the mistakes brought about by other people. Of course, I assess the situation wrongly too. A plant does not do equally well on any type of soil. On rich clay soil, a plant will grow taller than on poor sandy soil. I take this into account. But I cannot influence the quantities of fertilizers which are used afterwards. This also has an effect on the height of the plants. When I use a particular plant, I picture a fully grown specimen which I have seen somewhere. In addition to that, I also still check the site beforehand to get the feel of where it stood. The plant could perhaps look totally different in a different place. It is always instructive to visit gardens which have been laid out a few years earlier.

Mistaken ornaments and materials

Garden statuary and garden furniture are very personal and for this reason I show in my plans only the site where they could be put. In spite of this, a mistaken choice of statue or incongruous furniture can spoil a garden plan considerably. Thus a small town garden calls for slim-line and light furniture, which is not necessarily comfortable for sitting on. Bulky, comfortable furniture made of plastic with cushions

Opposite:
The garden path is 2m (6ft) wide. As the plants grow, the path will look narrower (design 1989).

When drawing up a garden plan, you need to know what plants the site is suitable for. Roses, for example, require a sunny and airy site and are there-fore not so suitable for enclosed town gar-dens. The photograph shows the single-flowered Rosa gallica *'Officinalis' (design 1989).*

which are much too thick is not suitable for such surroundings. Unfortunately, the designer has no influence on wrongly chosen items which are introduced later. The awful thing is that later he will probably be blamed for these failures!

Experiments Every garden plan must have something new in it. According to many, the garden paths are far too wide and the structures far too high when the garden is first laid out; experience has shown me that these dimensions do in actual fact come right once the garden is fully-grown, but some patience is required at first. With new developments, you cannot go by your experience; you never know how the material or the plant will turn out. But to make progress, you will, however, always have to come up with something new. But experimenting cannot be done at the expense of something else. When using forms or materials whose sturdiness or durability is not known, things must be thought out clearly in advance, so that the client can weigh up the risks.

Serendipity When designing a garden, you are sometimes handed things on a plate, such as unplanned vistas or reflections in the water which have an enlarging effect. Touching up a few things on the plan or changing the water level of a pond a bit can sometimes achieve a new effect. By pruning a tree, and with a little intervention in a planting scheme further away, a new image-defining view point can be achieved which can be reinforced by means of a statue.

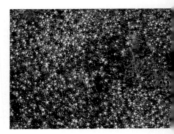

If cut back, Campanula porten- schlagiana *has a second flowering and is semi-evergreen.*

By raising a set of steps, a grass verge can be removed from view, thus creating a new effect. One change often paves the way to another. Many beautiful coincidences seem to come about with little planning; the unsuccessful risks are then really not so noticeable. It is often where everything is done strictly according to the plan, where it seems that nothing has been left to chance, that the most happy surprises occur.

Reflections, the I use many methods to try to make the surface area of the garden look
fourth dimension as large as possible by means of false perspectives, vistas, structures, and so on. A reflecting effect can also be an enlarging one. A classical example of this is the crystal ball or garden mirror. Tables can be made of glass, which makes a small space look as though it is not completely full up.

In the seventeenth century, Le Nôtre was already busy using mobile water containers to reproduce just the right reflections. The height of the water level is very important for a good reflection.

It was not only in the Baroque and Rococo periods, but also during the Classical period that hardly any water plants were used in formal ponds as these would have caused the reflections in the water to be lost.

Reflection also has an effect on the light: greenhouses in botanical gardens often stand behind a pond. The light from the reflecting surface of the water is used in this way to benefit the plants in the greenhouse, especially in winter.

A clearing in a wood is alluring. This is also applicable for the garden: light and shade give an effect of depth. After dense planting, the clearing which follows must be large enough for the sun to be able to shine on the ground.

Troublesome terminology

It seems to me that many amateurs do not know what a permanent plant is. When designing a permanent plant border, I therefore always first ask whether a shrub is also a permanent plant. In 50 per cent of cases, I receive an answer in the affirmative. I often therefore have to explain that permanent plants are herb-like, usually flowering plants which die back in the autumn and come up again in the spring. Shrubs and house-plants are admittedly permanent, but they are not permanent plants in the botanical sense.

The difference between hornbeam and beech, thus between a hornbeam hedge and a beech hedge, is such a great problem that many people must now be saddled with mixed hedges. To get an "unmixed" hedge, the scientific names must be used: *Carpinus betulus* (hornbeam) and *Fagus sylvatica* (beech).

It seems strange to many people that a shrub is not a permanent plant, but it is still a mystery to me what people imagine conifers to be. "No, we don't like conifers," and then they come out of the house with a

If well-situated, an ornament can have just as much effect in a garden as a complete flower border (design 1991).

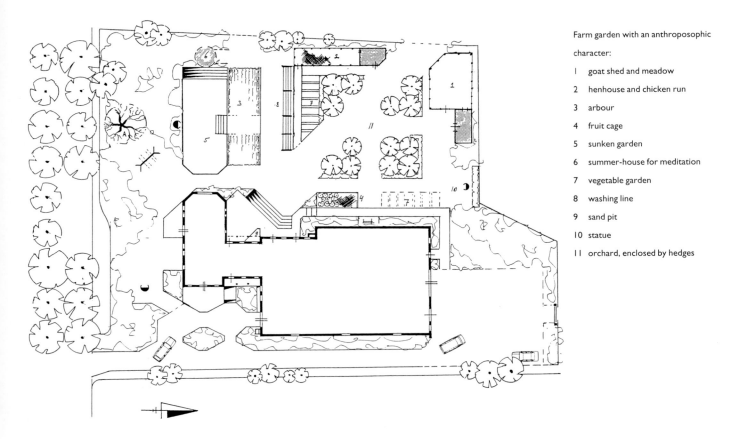

Farm garden with an anthroposophic

character:

1   goat shed and meadow

2   henhouse and chicken run

3   arbour

4   fruit cage

5   sunken garden

6   summer-house for meditation

7   vegetable garden

8   washing line

9   sand pit

10   statue

11   orchard, enclosed by hedges

bowl of fresh juniper berries. It is often terribly important to give people clear explanations. The word evergreen is often associated with conifers, which is not necessarily the case. As an adviser, it is better to avoid the word *Prunus*, even when referring to the common plum tree.

The cherry laurel again provides a great many difficulties: if I call it *Prunus*, people buy a Japanese flowering cherry and if I call it cherry laurel, people buy a bay laurel tree. This example illustrates clearly that correct and accurate use of scientific names is not unnecessary.

Advice on maintenance   People often ask for a maintenance-free or, better still, a low-maintenance garden. As a rule, as a landscape architect, I do not have to take this demand too seriously. Low-maintenance gardens are, after all, just a fashion and are certainly not a special feature of a garden. The reason why so many people ask for a maintenance-free garden is that they cannot face the maintenance.

In actual fact, the maintenance usually turns out to be easier than expected. A lot of time can be saved if you are a bit organized about the work. The time thus saved can be spent on weeding. A gardener would be too expensive? Let this man do the real professional jobs. The whole garden will be trimmed in a couple of hours if he comes once a year. You can save money by clearing away the branches yourself, if that takes more time than the pruning.

Weeds Perennial weeds which spread underground cause the greatest problems. People seem to worry about them much more than is necessary. The ground elder *(Aegopodium podograria)* is many people's bugbear. In a very neglected garden, make sure that the plant cannot spread again by removing the flowers immediately. The task is then to prevent the plant from forming chlorophyll: pick off or weed out the leaves. You do not have to dig down deep, but only a little way, and do not miss a single leaf. This job should, of course, be done with a very sharp spade.

If you repeat this process every two weeks during the season, the plant will not return in the following year. It soon looks as though the newly-formed leaf is getting smaller, but this is no reason to stop weeding and plucking! Never try to dig up the rhizomes: the little bits of root which are then left in the soil propagate the plant all over again, as the short pieces of rootstock will produce young plants again.

Up-keep of flower-beds and paths is important. Weeding must be done before weeds get the chance to spread their seed again. If you have a bad back, use the chemical sprayer. In a prolonged damp spell, it is pretty well impossible to avoid using it. Keep its use to a minimum, but if the weed threatens to overrun everything, you will have to take steps quickly to prevent having years of trouble due to the germinating seeds.

Stark lines.
A construction using
plum trees stands
where the axes cross
(design 1992/1995).

Common requests
and questions

In blocks of colour

A garden in blocks of colour is a frequent request. This is no hindrance at all to the landscape designer. It is very simple to leave out the red, yellow, and orange colours, which admittedly do not occur so often. The remaining colours always ensure harmony in the garden.

Yellow is usually seen as a spring colour, as most yellow blooms flower in the spring. A grey-white flower-bed is only suitable for drier and sunny gardens, so that it is not always possible to comply with this wish. The "grey" is made up of small fine hairs on the foliage to prevent the foliage from being scorched. For me, colour is only a very small part in the great spectrum of demands. Also, if a couple of "wrong colours" do occur in the garden, it is all the more obvious that great thought has gone into the other plants!

Herb gardens

A herb garden must be right by the house. I like to comply with the wishes of the occupants, but I will resist this demand with all the powers of persuasion I can muster. As a rule, kitchen herbs are the ugliest plants in the garden; in addition to this, a very large proportion of them are killed by frost each year. A bare or drab-looking section of the garden is the result. Kitchen herbs are not usually included in my garden plants: they are too much a matter of personal taste and people can always find an unobtrusive spot in the garden, preferably right by the vegetable garden, if there is one.

Formal clipped yew pathways combined with free-growing acacia trees (design 1991).

Town garden with pond
A gate in the hedge gives a view from the
terrace by the house to the middle of a
rectangular pond. A friendly attitude with
regard to the neighbours is created by not
fully enclosing the garden with fences and
hedges on both sides.

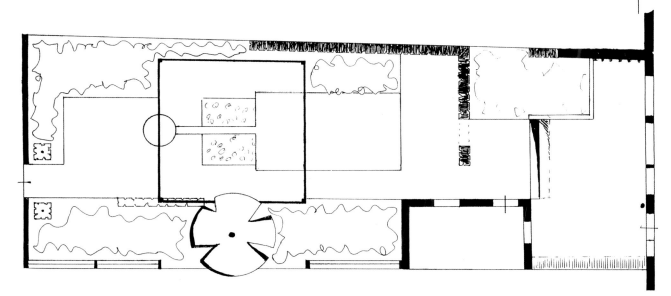

No fruit   The question of whether or not fruit should be grown in the garden is always considered in the planting schemes. I am often told that there must be no currant bushes, as the birds just eat up the berries. To my mind, that is exactly why a lot of currant bushes should be planted. Sound adds an extra dimension to a garden and currant bushes are exactly what the blackbird needs to give it the energy to make itself heard from a tree top in the evening!

Subsidies   In the case of plantings for estates, I am often asked whether there is any possibility of receiving a subsidy. Sometimes this is indeed the case. I shall, however, make one comment here. An application often takes a long time to be processed, which leads to a delay in planting. Waiting for a year means that planting will have become more expensive due to the higher prices of the plants and rising labour costs. If you are prepared to meet the demands of the grant-giving body, you often have to adapt the assortment of plants. Having the garden planted by a much more expensive cultivation company also incurs much higher costs. You therefore have to ask yourself whether applying for a subsidy really is such an attractive prospect.

Start straight away   After moving house, many people first make a start on making alterations to the house. I would advise you to start with the garden, as it takes a number of years for the garden to become fully grown. I hope that this book will give you the necessary inspiration.

Every pond should have Pontederia cordata.

Following page:
Saxifraga cortusifolia
'Rubrifolia'.
In addition to the reddish-brown foliage, this plant also has reddish-brown flower stalks.

141

*I dedicate this book to the gardeners who have implemented the
designs discussed in this book and by so doing
have brought them to life.*

© 1996 Zuid Boekprodukties, Lisse
© 1997 Published by Rebo Productions Ltd
2nd print 1997
Garden designs: Studio voor Tuinconsult
(Garden Consultancy)
Plans: Reitse A. Terpstra, Winsum, J.H. Gerritsen, Howerzijl
Cover design and lay-out: Ton Wienbelt, The Netherlands
Photographic editor: TextCase, The Netherlands
Production: TextCase, The Netherlands
Translation: Harriet Horsfield for First Edition Translations Ltd, Great Britain
Typesetting: Hof&Land Typografie, The Netherlands

ISBN 1 901094 44 8

Photographic credits

Ton Broekhuis, Groningen: pp. 56, 62, 65 below, 71, 72, 73 below, 132

E. de Jager, Vierhuizen: pp. 123 above, 125 above

C. van Mourik, Groningen: pp. 70, 73 above, 75 below, 79

Klaas T. Noordhuis, Leens: pp. 8 above, 9, 10, 11 above, 14 below, 24 right, 25, 26, 31, 32-33, 35, 36, 37 above, 38, 39 left and below, 82, 86, 94 right, 110 above, 119, 120, 121, 122, 123 below, 129, 130, 133 left, 142

Henk Reitsma, Den Andel: pp. 5, 6, 7, 8 below, 11 below, 12, 13, 14 above, 15, 16, 20, 21, 22 left, 23, 24 left, 27, 29, 34, 37 below, 39 right, 40, 41, 42, 43, 44, 45, 47, 50, 54, 55, 57, 65 above, 67, 68-69, 74, 75 above, 88, 89 left, 94 left, 96, 98, 99, 100, 103, 110 below, 112, 113, 114, 125 below, 126, 127, 133 right, 134, 135, 136, 137, 139, 140, 141

Peter Schut, Haarlem: pp. 18, 22 right, 48, 53, 59, 60, 76, 77, 80-81, 87, 89 right, 101, 102, 105, 106, 107, 109, 115, 116, 117, 118

Gerben Wynia, Hengelo: p. 91